CIMA

E X A M   P R A C T I C E   K I T

MANAGEMENT LEVEL

PAPER E2

PROJECT AND RELATIONSHIP
MANAGEMENT

FOR EXAMS IN 2017

BPP
LEARNING MEDIA

Third edition October 2016

ISBN 9781 5097 0701 0
e-ISBN 9781 5097 0734 8

British Library Cataloguing-in-Publication Data
A catalogue record for this book
is available from the British Library

Published by

BPP Learning Media Ltd
BPP House, Aldine Place, 142/144 Uxbridge Road
London W12 8AA

www.bpp.com/learningmedia

Printed in the United Kingdom by

Wheatons Exeter Ltd
Hennock Road
Marsh Barton
Exeter
EX2 8RP

Your learning materials, published by BPP Learning Media
Ltd, are printed on paper obtained from traceable,
sustainable sources.

BPP
LEARNING MEDIA

Contents

Question and Answer index

Using your BPP Exam Practice Kit

One of the key criteria for achieving exam success is question practice. There is generally a direct correlation between candidates who study all topics and practise exam questions and those who are successful in their real exams. This Kit gives you ample opportunity for such practice throughout your preparations for your OT exam.

All questions in your exam are compulsory and all the component learning outcomes will be examined so you must **study the whole syllabus**. Selective studying will limit the number of questions you can answer and hence reduce your chances of passing. It is better to go into the exam knowing a reasonable amount about most of the syllabus rather than concentrating on a few topics to the exclusion of the rest.

Practising as many exam-style questions as possible will be the key to passing this exam. You must do questions under **timed conditions**.

Breadth of question coverage

Questions will cover the whole of the syllabus so you must study all the topics in the syllabus.

The weightings in the table below indicate the approximate proportion of study time you should spend on each topic, and is related to the number of questions per syllabus area in the exam.

E2 Project and Relationship Management Syllabus topics	Weighting
A Introduction to strategic management and assessing the global environment	30%
B The human aspects of the organisation	20%
C Managing relationships	20%
D Managing change through projects	30%

The Objective Test exam

The Objective Test exam is a computer based assessment, which is available on demand at assessment centres all year round.

Objective Test exams in each level can be taken in any order, but candidates must pass all the OT exams for a level before they can sit the Integrated Case Study Exam for that level.

Each exam lasts for 90 minutes and the pass mark is 70%.

Results are available shortly after the test has been completed, and the results will include feedback.

The exam will be made up of different types of questions, including:

Question Type	Explanation
Multiple choice	Standard multiple choice items provide four options. 1 option is correct and the other 3 are incorrect. Incorrect options will be plausible, so you should expect to have to use detailed, syllabus-specific knowledge to identify the correct answer rather than relying on common sense.
Multiple response	A multiple response item is the same as a multiple choice question, except more than one response is required. You will normally (but not always) be told how many options you need to select.
Drag and drop	Drag and drop questions require you to drag a 'token' onto a pre-defined area. These tokens can be images or text. This type of question is effective at testing the order of events, labelling a diagram or linking events to outcomes.
Gap fill	Gap fill (or 'fill in the blank') questions require you to type a short numerical response. You should carefully follow the instructions in the question in terms of how to type your answer – eg the correct number of decimal places.
Hot spot	These questions require you to identify an area or location on an image by clicking on it. This is commonly used to identify a specific point on a graph or diagram
Drop-down list	Drop-down lists follow the same principle as multiple choice questions, in that you need to select one option from a pre-defined list. This can be used in conjunction with a gap-fill question: for example, you may be asked to key a numerical answer into a gap-fill box and then select an explanation for the approach you've taken from a drop-down list.

Learning Objectives

The table below has been prepared by CIMA to help you understand the abilities that CIMA is seeking to assess.

Learning objective	Verbs used	Definition	Example question types
1 Knowledge			
What you are expected to know	• List	• Make a list of	MCQ
	• State	• Express, fully or clearly, the details of/facts of	MCQ
	• Define	• Give the exact meaning of	MCQ
2 Comprehension			
What you are expected to understand	• Describe	• Communicate the key features of	Multiple Response
	• Distinguish	• Highlight the differences between	Multiple Response
	• Explain	• Make clear or intelligible/state the meaning or purpose of	Drop down list
	• Identify	• Recognise, establish or select after consideration	Hotspot
	• Illustrate	• Use an example to describe or explain something	Drop down list
3 Application			
How you are expected to apply your knowledge	• Apply	• Put to practical use	Multiple response
	• Calculate/ compute	• Ascertain or reckon mathematically	Number entry
	• Demonstrate	• Prove the certainty or exhibit by practical means	Hotspot
	• Prepare	• Make or get ready for use	Drag and drop
	• Reconcile	• Make or prove consistent/ compatible	Drop down list
	• Solve	• Find an answer to	Number entry
	• Tabulate	• Arrange in a table	Drag and drop
4 Analysis			
How you are expected to analyse the detail of what you have learned	• Analyse	• Examine in detail the structure of	Multiple response
	• Categorise	• Place into a defined class or division	Drag and drop
	• Compare & contrast	• Show the similarities and/or differences between	Hotspot
	• Construct	• Build up or complete	Drag and drop
	• Discuss	• Examine in detail by argument	Multiple response
	• Interpret	• Translate into intelligible or familiar terms	Multiple response
	• Prioritise	• Place in order of priority or sequence for action	Drop down list
	• Produce	• Create or bring into existence	Drag and drop

Learning objective	Verbs used	Definition	Example question types
5 Evaluation			
How you are expected to use your learning to evaluate, make decisions or recommendations	• Advise	• Counsel, inform or notify	Multiple response
	• Evaluate	• Appraise or assess the value of	Multiple response
	• Recommend	• Propose a course of action	Multiple response

In your CBA, questions will be set which test up to the cognitive level of the verb in the component learning outcome in each paper's syllabus, so this means they will test up to level 5 verbs where the learning outcome permits this.

CIMA will limit the number of lower level questions in the exam – so that students will not be able to achieve the pass mark solely based on correctly answering knowledge and comprehension questions. Higher level questions, requiring candidates to demonstrate application, analysis and evaluation skills must be answered correctly for the pass mark to be reached.

BPP LEARNING MEDIA

Passing the E2 Objective Test exam

Tackling OTQs

- Read, and **re-read the question** to ensure you fully understand what is being asked.

- When starting to read a question, especially one with a lengthy scenario, **read the requirement first**. You will then find yourself considering the requirement as you read the data in the scenario, helping you to focus on exactly what you have to do.

- **Do not spend too much time on one question** – remember you should spend 1½ minutes, on average, per question

- If you cannot decide between two answers – look carefully and decide whether for one of the options you are making an unnecessary assumption – **do not be afraid of trusting your gut instinct**.

- **Do not keep changing your mind** – research has shown that the 1st answer that appeals to you is often the correct one.

- Remember that marks are awarded for correct answers, and marks will not be deducted for incorrect answers. Therefore **answer every single question**, even ones you are unsure of.

- Always submit an answer for a given question even if you do not know the answer – **never leave any answers blank**

- **Pace yourself** – you will need to work through the exam at the right speed. Too fast and your accuracy may suffer, too slow and you may run out of time. Use this Kit to practice your time keeping and approach to answering each question.

- If you are unsure about anything, remember to **ask the test administrator** before the test begins. Once the clock begins ticking, interruptions will not be allowed

- Remember to **keep moving on!** You may be presented with a question which you simply cannot answer due to difficulty or if the wording is too vague. If you have only approximately 90 seconds per question, and you find yourself spending five minutes determining the answer for a question then your time management skills are poor and you are wasting valuable time.

- If you finish the exam with time to spare, use the rest of the time to **review your answers** and to make sure that you answered every OTQ.

Demonstrating your understanding of E2

The E2 examiner will expect you to demonstrate the following:

Application is important	You must be able to **identify, apply** and **analyse** key issues in a variety of question scenarios.
Use your strategy, management and project knowledge	You must be confident in explaining different approaches that management can employ to help the entity deliver its strategy or project successfully. You are encouraged to use your knowledge of the various theoretical models you have seen as part of your E2 studies when attempting questions.
Think about the context of the question	When reading through the scenario questions you need to think widely about the strategy of the organisation featured, the management styles of those characters mentioned and the controls the organisation uses in order to operate.
Show management awareness	Remember this is a Management level paper, so there is a strong focus on people. Always think about the practical implications that business decisions have on people.

All OTQs in all the exams are worth the same number of marks, both in this Kit and in the real exam. However, this is an approximate guide: some OTQs are very short and just require a factual selection, which you either know or you don't, while others are more complex, which will inevitably take more time. Note that the real exam will be balanced such that the 'difficulty' of the exam will be fair for all students – the OTQs in this Kit have also been balanced in a similar way.

Using the solutions and feedback

Avoid looking at the answer until you have finished a question. It can be very tempting to do so, but unless you give the question a proper attempt under exam conditions you will not know how you would have coped with it in the real exam scenario.

When you do look at the answer, compare it with your own and give some thought to why your answer was different, if it was.

If you did not reach the correct answer make sure that you work through the explanation or workings provided, to see where you went wrong. If you think that you do not understand the principle involved, work through and revise the point again, to ensure that you will understand it if it occurs in the exam.

Objective Test questions

1a Introduction to strategy

1a.1 Tim Company bases its competitive advantage on identifying activities that are imperfectly imitable.

This approach is referred to as:

☐   The positioning approach
☐   The ecological approach
☐   The resource-based approach
☐   The outside-in approach

1a.2 Sabrina Airways has an excellent reputation and brand image. This is achieved through investing in staff training and development to ensure customers receive the highest level of service.

Where in the value chain is Sabrina Airways adding value?

☐   Technology development, marketing and sales, outbound logistics
☐   Marketing and sales, outbound logistics, human resource management
☐   Firm infrastructure, marketing and sales, human resource management
☐   Human resource management, marketing and sales, service

1a.3 All companies need processes or activities that they must be good at just to be considered by a potential customer.

These are referred to as which of the following?

☐   Core competences
☐   Threshold resources
☐   Unique capabilities
☐   Threshold competences

1a.4 **Corporate strategy is concerned with which of the following?**

Select ALL that apply.

☐   Marketing decisions on price
☐   Decisions to enter new markets
☐   Routine decisions
☐   Production decisions
☐   Complex decisions
☐   Relations with external stakeholders
☐   Distribution decisions

1a.5 Write the types of strategy into the correct boxes in the diagram below to illustrate Mintzberg's emergent approach to strategy formulation.

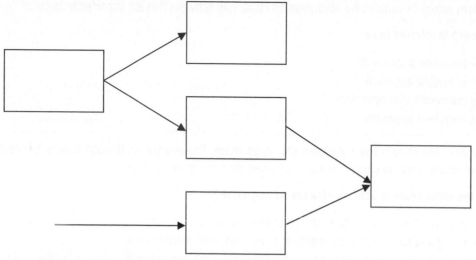

(a) Emergent strategy
(b) Realised strategy
(c) Deliberate strategy
(d) Unrealised strategy
(e) Intended strategy

1a.6 **In comparison to the formal planning approach to strategy development, the emergent approach is associated with which THREE of the following?**

☐ Visionary entrepreneurs
☐ Goal congruence
☐ A response to unexpected contingencies
☐ The belief that reliable assumptions can be made about the future
☐ Strategy can be tried and developed as it is implemented

1a.7 HKG Company is a manufacturer and retailer of luxury products including watches, jewellery and handbags. It has recently undertaken a corporate appraisal as part of its annual planning cycle.

From the external and internal analysis it has identified a number of factors which will have implications for its future strategy direction.

For each factor indicate if it is an opportunity, threat, strength or weakness, by writing each factor into the correct position in the table.

(a) Political risk in a county where HKG exports to
(b) Over reliance on external providers of quality raw materials
(c) Excellent product design
(d) Global economic recovery

Strength	Weakness
Opportunity	Threat

1a.8 There are many different definitions of strategy. Mintzberg suggests various definitions using five 'P's.

Complete the boxes by writing the 'P' from the list below next to the correct definition.

    (a)   Perspective
    (b)   Position
    (c)   Ploy
    (d)   Pattern
    (e)   Plan

Definition	**Insert correct 'P'**
Strategy is a unique way of perceiving the world, interpreting information and judging opportunities and choices. Different organisations might respond to environmental stimulus in different ways.	
Strategy involves manoeuvres to outclass competitors and can be viewed as a competitive business game.	

1a.9 **Write the following terms in the boxes, to show the correct hierarchy of goal structure (1 = the highest level) for strategy development.**

    (a)   Key Performance Indicators
    (b)   Vision
    (c)   Mission
    (d)   Goals
    (e)   Objectives

1.	
2.	
3.	
4.	
5.	

1a.10 When compared with the resource-based approach the positioning approach to strategy:

Select THREE options.

- ☐ is outside-in
- ☐ is based on core competences
- ☐ ensures the organisation has a good fit with its environment
- ☐ focuses on what the organisation does best
- ☐ assumes the future of markets is predictable

1b Contemporary perspectives in strategy development

1b.1 CK Company, which specialises in knitwear, has identified that in order to achieve its diversification strategy it will need to form a relationship with another company. The target is a company called Wooldn't You Like To Know and CK intends to establish a legal contract to cooperate in defined ways to achieve specific objectives.

This is known as which of the following?

- ☐ Merger
- ☐ Outsourcing
- ☐ Strategic alliance
- ☐ Network organisation

1b.2 **Which of the below statements are true of transaction costs?**

Select ALL that apply.

- ☐ Transaction cost theory allows distinctive competences to be identified
- ☐ Transaction cost theory supports organisational restructuring
- ☐ IT increases transaction costs
- ☐ Increased trust increases transaction costs

1b.3 **The characteristics of an emerging economy include which THREE of the following?**

- ☐ Rapid economic growth
- ☐ Decline in manufacturing and associated increase in agricultural employment
- ☐ Overall improvement in living standards
- ☐ Increasing economic equality among citizens
- ☐ Increasing urbanisation

1b.4 **What is the main difference between an acquisition and a merger?**

- ☐ Acquisitions are paid for in cash but mergers are paid for in shares
- ☐ Acquisitions involve one entity subsuming another but a merger is a meeting on equal terms
- ☐ Acquisitions are always hostile but mergers are always mutual
- ☐ Acquisitions are always mutual but mergers are always hostile

1b.5   Objectives in the not-for-profit sector are usually focussed around the three E's of economy, efficiency and effectiveness.

CAT is a charity for the protection and re-homing of cats. For each of the following calculations carried out by CAT, state whether they address objectives related to economy, efficiency or effectiveness.

(i)   Economy
(ii)   Efficiency
(iii) Effectiveness

Annual spend on veterinary fees

Number of cats re-homed this month

Average cost per animal per week

1b.6   El Jefe is considering outsourcing its business support services (finance, and marketing which is largely social media-based). The Chief Financial Officer, Jon, has expressed concern about reducing costs and maintaining a robust level of governance over the work of the finance and marketing functions.

Which of the following will apply to the company in terms of transaction costs and control if the outsourcing option is adopted?

☐   Low transaction costs and low control
☐   High transaction costs and low control

1b.7   As ecological issues have become a more pressing concern for companies in the modern business environment, the ecological perspective of strategy has evolved.

Match the six ecological areas that need to be monitored to its description:

(i)   Production
(ii)   Environmental auditing
(iii) Ecological approach
(iv)   Quality
(v)   Accounting
(vi)   Economic

Minimising inputs required to generate outputs

Compliance with legislation, treatment of waste etc.

Trace the full life-cycle of the product

A TQM approach to continuous improvement

Shadow pricing to quantify environmental consequences

Environmental cost allocated to relevant processes

1b.8   Ghoshal & Bartlett suggested that firms can replace traditional organisational structures with a network or virtual structure and buy in those value-adding activities they require.

Which one of the following does NOT support that suggestion?

☐   Capital assets can be leased
☐   Ability to outsource certain activities
☐   Legislation to make it easier to hire and fire employees
☐   Staff can be hired on a contract basis

1b.9 Company IEO has decided to make product BAC in its home country. The product is patented overseas but Company IEO has the exclusive rights to make product BAC independently for a period of three years under its own brand name.

This is an example of which one of the following?

☐ Franchising
☐ Joint venture
☐ Consortium
☐ Licensing

1b.10 **Match each term with its definition.**

(i) globalisation
(ii) glocalisation
(iii) internationalisation

An emphasis on customising products and services to fit local conditions ⬜

Functional integration of internationally dispersed activities ⬜

Extension of trade beyond national/economic/political boundaries ⬜

2 General environment

2.1 **Which of the following characteristics create high barriers to entry to an industry?**

Select ALL that apply.

☐ Low number of rivals
☐ High level of differentiation
☐ High entry costs
☐ Low mobility barriers
☐ Low cost structure
☐ Strong brand presence
☐ Highly vertically integrated firms

2.2 TWS Company owns a national chain of supermarkets in Country V. It has a strong brand in the marketplace, along with four other leading supermarket chains. Whilst the company deals with a number of different suppliers, its business represents a high proportion of the suppliers' total sales.

With reference to Porter's five forces model, determine the power of suppliers for TWS and the nature of barriers to entry. Write the correct levels into the box below:

High
Medium
Low

Power of suppliers ⬜

Barriers to entry ⬜

2.3 Match the following economic tools and indicators with the relevant type of government policy.

(i)   Fiscal policy
(ii) Monetary policy

Control of the money supply
:selected:

Interest rates

Government spending

Exchange rates

Government borrowing

2.4 Which of the following would you consider to be relevant to the social part of the LoNGPEST model?

Select ALL that apply.

- :unselected: Effect of unemployment on demand
- :unselected: Changes in safety legislation
- :unselected: Changes in leisure pursuits
- :unselected: Analysis of the population by age group
- :unselected: Volatility of interest rates
- :unselected: Religious affiliation and practices

2.5 Porter's analysis of the competitive advantage of nations identified basic and advanced factor conditions that contribute to the success of a nation in producing a particular good or service.

Which of the following are basic factors and which are advanced?

(i)   Advanced factor
(ii) Basic factor

Higher education system

Up to date telecommunications networks

Access to diverse coastline and complex river systems

Access to road and rail systems

2.6 Which of the following may be considered a substitute product for an airline providing business class flights?

Select ALL that apply.

- :unselected: Low cost airline
- :unselected: Video conferencing
- :unselected: A different airline providing business class flights
- :unselected: A different airline providing first class flights
- :unselected: High-speed international train link

2.7 In Italy the leather footwear industry, the leather working machinery industry and the design services which underpin them benefit from one another.

To which part of Porter's Diamond does this relate to?

- :unselected: Related and supporting industries
- :unselected: Factor conditions
- :unselected: Firm strategy, structure and rivalry
- :unselected: Demand conditions

2.8 **Which of the following is not a benefit of globalisation?**

☐ Flexibility to move production to lower cost market
☐ Elimination of business risk due to geographical diversification
☐ Potential access to profitable markets
☐ Economies of scale

2.9 **Match the following impacts on a company's bargaining power in relation to its customers with the list of triggers.**

Impact

(i) No impact
(ii) Increase bargaining power of the seller
(iii) Decrease bargaining power of the seller

Trigger	Impact
The company's products are successfully differentiated through branding	
The company's customers are signed up to long-term contracts and must pay a penalty if they terminate the contract early	
The company's suppliers are signed up to long-term contracts and must pay a penalty if they terminate the contract early	
There has been a trend toward mergers between the company's customers	

2.10 **Which of the following will definitely not lower barriers to entry into an industry?**

Select ALL that apply.

☐ Technological changes
☐ New distribution channels
☐ Changes in the political environment
☐ Increase in patent protection
☐ Requirement for firms in the industry to invest in land and computers

3 Competitive environment

3.1 **In comparison with quantitative research, qualitative research is associated with which THREE of the following?**

☐ A focus on 'why' questions rather than 'what' 'where' and 'when'.
☐ The selection and discussion of only ratios that have a direct impact on the company.
☐ Costly to undertake.
☐ An emphasis on gathering non-financial data such as the number of customers entering a store
☐ The attempt to find out customer preferences for our products rather than for our competitors products.

3.2 **The role of competitor analysis includes which THREE of the following:**

☐ It helps managers to understand their company's competitive advantages/disadvantages as compared with competitors

☐ It helps copy-cat strategic behaviour

☐ It aids understanding of competitors' past, present and future behaviour

☐ It provides an informed basis to assist a company to develop its own competitive strategies

☐ It provides a basis for entering another industry

3.3 Kotler identifies four levels of competitors.

Write the correct labels against the descriptions to show the different levels of competitors.

(a) Generic
(b) Brand
(c) Form
(d) Industry

Description	
Firms whose products satisfy the same needs although they are technically quite different	
Firms who compete for the same income, but offer different products	
Firms who have similar products, the same customers and are of a similar size	
Firms who produce similar products but who are different in size or structure or compete in a more limited area/product range	

3.4 Company DIL makes domestic household security alarms for affluent homeowners. In order to grow its business it has decided to pursue two strategies.

Match the strategic direction from Ansoff's matrix to the two strategies below.

(i) Price skimming
(ii) Market development
(iii) Price Penetration
(iv) Strategic alliance
(v) Market penetration
(vi) Diversification
(vii) Product development
(viii) Takeover

Selling the same alarms, albeit with different casings, to smaller, less affluent households for a lower price.

Development of new, more sophisticated alarms and a wide range of security services (guards and surveillance) for sale to industrial clients for higher prices.

3.5 **State whether the following statements are true or false?**

Cost leadership strategies involve striving to be the lowest price seller in the industry as a whole.

According to Porter a cost leadership strategy may be successfully pursued in conjunction with a focus strategy.

According to Porter a cost leadership strategy may be successfully pursued in conjunction with one of differentiation.

3.6 **Match the following competitor reactions to the explanations.**

(i) Laid back
(ii) Selective
(iii) Tiger
(iv) Stochastic

The firm reacts strongly to certain types of competitive attacks

The firm does not remain quiet and reacts strongly to any attack on its markets or products

The firm does not exhibit any predictable reaction pattern

3.7 **Complete the second paragraph using the available words:**

- form
- industry
- generic
- tiger
- selective

VTT operates in a limited geographical area. For many years there was no significant competition. Recently a new competitor, FID, has been established delivering the same service as VTT. FID is smaller than VTT but has discounted its prices significantly on a number of occasions in its first year. VTT cut its prices just as significantly each time and responded with a vibrant marketing campaign.

VTT and FID are _____ level competitors and VTT shows itself to be a _____ competitor in reaction to the competitive threat.

3.8 **Complete the following paragraph using the available words:**

- Big data
- Benchmarking
- Uncorrelated
- Structured
- Trends
- Uncertainty

_____ is a term used to describe the extraction of meaning from vast quantities of _____ data. Organisations are particularly interested in identifying _____ and correlations in the data that they collect and store with the aim of putting this to commercial use.

3.9 **In the context of the Boston Consulting Group matrix which of the following were not used as classifications?**

Select ALL that apply.

☐ Lions
☐ Dogs
☐ Cash cows
☐ Question marks
☐ Stars
☐ Problem children
☐ Silos

3.10 **Match the terms with their definitions.**

   (i) Environmental scanning
   (ii) Qualitative research
   (iii) Strategic intelligence

The process of gathering external information which is available from a wide range of sources

What an organisation needs to know about its business environment to enable it to anticipate change and design appropriate strategies that will create business value for customers

Collection and analysis of non-numerical data

4a Key concepts in management

4a.1 **What is the key contribution of the human relations approach to management?**

   ☐ Awareness of the importance of group dynamics and worker attitudes as an influence on productivity
   ☐ Concern for productivity and efficiency
   ☐ Awareness of the many different variables that influence and constrain a manager's behaviour
   ☐ Proof of a clear link between job satisfaction, worker motivation and business success

4a.2 **Of Mintzberg's managerial roles, which is being exercised by a manager who gathers information from contacts within and outside the organisation?**

   ☐ Leader
   ☐ Monitor
   ☐ Spokesperson
   ☐ Disseminator

4a.3 **Which of the following are part of Peter Drucker's five categories of the work of managers?**

   Select ALL that apply.

   ☐ Managing a business
   ☐ The job of measurement
   ☐ Managing managers
   ☐ Motivating
   ☐ Developing people

4a.4 **Handy's Shamrock would be appropriate as an organisational structure for which of the following organisations?**

   Select ALL that apply.

   ☐ A large accountancy practice
   ☐ An airline
   ☐ A small retail store
   ☐ A design agency
   ☐ A sports team
   ☐ A sole trader making bespoke furniture

4a.5 **A process of Management By Objectives will be effective if it involves which of the following?**

Select ALL that apply.

- ☐ Reviewed only once a year
- ☐ Targets set are measurable
- ☐ Resources are scarce
- ☐ Continual review of results
- ☐ Staff jointly set objectives with managers
- ☐ Goals are incongruent
- ☐ Goals are stated in behavioural terms

4a.6 **Which of the following is an 'interpersonal' role of management, in Mintzberg's classification of managerial roles?**

- ☐ Spokesperson
- ☐ Figurehead
- ☐ Negotiator
- ☐ Resource allocator

4a.7 **Which major sub-system, according to Trist and Bamforth, is the more dominant at WPW Company before and after technology was introduced?**

Match each of the roles against the description of WPW Company.

(i) Social Systems
(ii) Technical Systems

At WPW there were small, integrated work groups consisting of a skilled man, his mate and one or two labourers. There was a high degree of autonomy at the work group level. The group was paid for its work as a group.

WPW then introduced new technology creating a need for larger, more specialised groups. A single cycle of mechanised production might extend over three shifts, each performing a separate process and made up of 10 to 20 men. Physical dispersion also greatly increased.

4a.8 **Select one of Burns and Stalker's organisational forms for each of the descriptions below.**

(i) Organic Organisations
(ii) Mechanic Organisations

Flexible and adaptive organisational forms

Stable and efficient organisational forms

Suitable for slow-changing operating environments

Suitable for dynamic operating environments

4a.9 **Which of the following are advantages of bureaucracy?**

Select ALL that apply.

- ☐ Communication is only through established channels, which increases suggestions made.
- ☐ They are ideal for standardised, routine tasks.
- ☐ Some people are suited to the structured, predictable environment.
- ☐ It results in fast decision making.
- ☐ They can enhance creativity, initiative and openness to new ideas and ways of doing things.
- ☐ Rigid adherence to procedures may be necessary for fairness, adherence to the law, safety and security.

4a.10 Sherwood Company employs 6,000 staff. Results from a recent staff survey suggest high levels of dissatisfaction, despite Mr Sherwood himself being a thoroughly decent chap. It is evident that some of the causes are related to hygiene factors and some to motivational factors.

Which of the following causes of dissatisfaction in Sherwood Company represent hygeine factors?

Select ALL that apply.

- ☐ Unpleasant working conditions
- ☐ Limited opportunities for career advancement
- ☐ Below market rate salary
- ☐ High levels of supervision and tight control
- ☐ No recognition of high performance
- ☐ Routine and boring work

4b Key concepts in leadership

4b.1 There are inevitable tensions involved in asserting staff authority. Technostructure is a term used by Mintzberg to describe individuals in the organisation who strive for efficiency and standardise work processes.

Write each of the possible solutions against the problem below.

(i) Technostructure experts should be involved in implementing their suggestions and share accountability for outcomes.

(ii) Use functional authority (via policies and procedures). Experts should be seen as a resource, not a threat.

(iii) Clear demarcations of line, staff and functional authority should be created.

(iv) Technostructure planners should be fully aware of operational issues, and communicate regularly with the middle line.

The technostructure can undermine the line managers' authority, by empire building.

Lack of seniority. Middle line managers may be more senior in the hierarchy than technostructure advisers.

Expert managers may lack realism, going for technically perfect but commercially impractical solutions.

Technostructure experts lack responsibility for the success of their ideas.

4b.2 **Choose from the following words to complete the sentence.**

- responsibility
- power
- accountability
- authority

Delegation is the process whereby a manager assigns part of his [   ] to a subordinate but the manager's [   ] can never be delegated.

4b.3 McGonagall, the Finance Director, has worked for HSWW for over 20 years and during that period many of her colleagues have commented that she is the best manager they have had and want to imitate her.

Which of the following best indicates the power source this gives McGonagall?

- ☐ Coercive
- ☐ Referent
- ☐ Reward
- ☐ Expert

4b.4 **Empowerment goes hand in hand with which of the following?**

Select ALL that apply.

- ☐ Knowledge workers
- ☐ Centralisation
- ☐ Flexibility
- ☐ Increasing middle management
- ☐ Top down management
- ☐ Delegation
- ☐ Delayering

4b.5 Daisy is a senior manager at Wow.com. She uses vision, example and persuasion to convince the group to pursue a new purpose. Colleagues have described her as possessing foresight. She understands and empathises with group members' needs, and will empower group members, so as to make the group more effective. She also has good self-understanding.

Daisy would be described as which type of leader?

- ☐ Transactional
- ☐ Transformational
- ☐ Entrepreneurial
- ☐ Trait
- ☐ Contingency
- ☐ Theory X

4b.6 Debbie is very busy perfecting her recipe for Potato Tart Tatin ahead of the launch of her new cookery book, but she also has to copy edit the rest of the recipes. She has a competent assistant, so her agent Doug told her she should delegate.

Which of the following are benefits of delegation?

Select ALL that apply.

- ☐ There are physical and mental limitations to the workload of any individual or group in authority.

- ☐ Managers are freed up to concentrate on higher-level tasks (such as recipe development).

- ☐ The increasing size and complexity of some organisations requires specialisation from both a managerial and technical perspective.

- ☐ Delegating authority contributes to the job satisfaction and development of the managers who delegate.

- ☐ Delegation shortens the chain of decision making, and brings decisions closer to the situations that require them.

- ☐ Delegation reduces the need for management to control the performance of employees as they perform more tasks themselves.

4b.7   There are three basic 'schools' of leadership theory.

Match the school of leadership against the description to which it applies.

(i)   Trait theories
(ii)   Style theories
(iii)   Contingency theories

Based on analysing the personality characteristics or preferences of successful leaders.

⬚

Based on the view that leadership is an interpersonal process whereby different leader behaviours influence people in different ways. More or less effective patterns of behaviour (or 'styles') can therefore be adopted.

⬚

Based on the belief that there is no 'one best way' of leading, but that effective leaders adapt their behaviour to specific and changing variables in the leadership context: the nature of the task, the personalities of team members, the organisation culture and so on.

⬚

4b.8   **Match the activity in the process of delegation next to the step to which it applies:**

(i)   Allocate resources and authority to the subordinate to enable them to carry out the delegated tasks at the expected level of performance.

(ii)   Formally assign tasks to the subordinate, who should formally agree to do them.

(iii)   Maintain contact, to review progress made, make constructive criticism and be available to give help and advice if requested.

(iv)   Specify performance in terms of the goals and standards expected of the subordinate, keeping in mind their level of expertise.

(v)   Back off and allow the subordinate to perform the delegated tasks.

Step 1   ⬚

Step 2   ⬚

Step 3   ⬚

Step 4   ⬚

Step 5   ⬚

4b.9   Max Weber proposed three ways in which managers exercised what he called legitimate power (or authority).

Match each of the types of power against the relevant description.

(i)   Rational-legal authority
(ii)   Traditional authority
(iii)   Charismatic authority

Authority arising from the personality of the leader and their ability to inspire devotion through, for example, sanctity, heroism or example.

⬚

Authority resting on established belief in the importance of immemorial tradition and the status it confers.

⬚

Authority arising from the working of accepted normative rules, such as are found in organisations and democratic governments.

⬚

4b.10 In practice, matters are rarely clear cut, and in many organisations responsibility and authority are ambiguous and shifting. This can result in mismatches of Authority and Responsibility.

Write each of the mismatches against the problem they cause below:

(i)   Authority without responsibility
(ii)   Responsibility without authority

This can lead to arbitrary and irresponsible behaviour, as the person has the right to make decisions without being held accountable for them.

```
┌──────────────────┐
│                  │
└──────────────────┘
```

This places a subordinate in an impossible and stressful position, as they are held accountable for results over which they have no control.

```
┌──────────────────┐
│                  │
└──────────────────┘
```

5 Culture

5.1   In Denison's analysis, there are four possible cultures.

Match the culture beside the organisation to which it applies.

(i)   Consistency culture
(ii)   Mission culture
(iii)   Adaptability culture
(iv)   Involvement culture

A large bread company exists in a stable environment, and its structure is well integrated. Management are preoccupied with efficiency with formal ways of behaviour.

```
┌──────────────────┐
│                  │
└──────────────────┘
```

Hospitals are preoccupied with the sick, inevitably their values are patient orientated and staff's work has meaning and value.

```
┌──────────────────┐
│                  │
└──────────────────┘
```

5.2   According to Schein, organisation culture exists at three different levels. Which of the following are included in the level 'artefacts and creations'?

Select ALL that apply.

☐   Beliefs of environmental issues
☐   Language
☐   Dress codes
☐   How people should be treated
☐   Office layout
☐   How people justify what they do
☐   Logos and branding

5.3   **Ouchi described the Theory J organisation (Japanese) as being characterised by which of the following?**

Select ALL that apply.

☐   Long-term employment, with slow progressing managerial career paths.
☐   Concern for employee focuses on work performance.
☐   Explicit controls, formal measures.
☐   Collective consensus decision-making processes.
☐   Industrial relations characterised by trust, co-operation and mutual adjustment.

5.4 **Which of Deal and Kennedy's corporate cultures applies best to Foutts, an exclusive bank accepting only the most affluent clients?**

☐ Process culture
☐ Bet your company culture
☐ Hard macho culture
☐ Work hard play hard culture

5.5 You are considering ways to make your business more successful and you have decided you want to reposition your organisation by offering unique levels of customer service in your industry. This change refers to the 'strategy' element of McKinsey's 7 S Model.

From the list below identify the most appropriate element of the McKinsey 7 S Model and write this beside the action to which it relates.

(i) Strategy
(ii) Structure
(iii) Staff
(iv) Skills
(v) Systems
(vi) Style
(vii) Shared values

You might have to set up team-working in customer-facing units to increase responsiveness.

☐

You may need to train people in customer service skills.

☐

They will also need new procedures and IT systems for better access to customer data.

☐

Managers will have to adjust to empowering staff, and new corporate image will be developed.

☐

5.6 **The cultural dimension that describes a cultural value where community is not a high priority is referred to by Hofstede as:**

☐ Individualism
☐ Collectivism
☐ Power distance
☐ Masculinity

5.7 **Ouchi described the Theory A organisation (American) as being characterised by which of the following?**

Select ALL that apply.

☐ Short-term employment with focus on specialisation of skills.

☐ Broad concern for employee welfare, both inside and outside the work context, i.e. commitment to the 'organisation family'.

☐ Implicit informal controls, such as guiding values.

☐ Individuals ultimately responsible for defined areas of accountability.

☐ Industrial relations characterised by trust, co-operation and mutual adjustment.

5.8   Deal and Kennedy consider cultures to be a function of which TWO of the following factors?

- ☐ Strategic orientation
- ☐ Willingness to take risk
- ☐ Environmental responses
- ☐ Management style
- ☐ Organisational structure
- ☐ Speed of feedback
- ☐ Company size

5.9   Match Denison's cultural type, beside the characteristics which apply.

(i)   Involvement culture
(ii)   Adaptability culture
(iii) Mission culture
(iv)   Consistency culture

This exists in a stable environment, and its structure is well integrated. Management are preoccupied with efficiency. Such cultures are characterised by formal ways of behaviour. Predictability and reliability are valued.

The environment is relatively stable, and the organisation is orientated towards it e.g. 'the customers'. Members' work activities are given meaning and value.

The basic premise is that the satisfaction of employees' needs is necessary for them to provide optimum performance. They take a 'human relations' approach to management.

The company's strategic focus is on the external environment, which is in a state of change. Corporate values encourage inquisitiveness and interest in the external environment.

5.10   The concept of supranational culture refers to which of the following?

- ☐ The superiority of one national culture
- ☐ The copying of national cultural characteristics
- ☐ The culture that extends across national boundaries
- ☐ The break-up of national cultures

6 Conflict, negotiation and communication

6.1   Which of the following statements about staff appraisals are true?

Select ALL that apply.

- ☐ They increase management control
- ☐ They can provide a fair basis for remuneration
- ☐ They enable succession planning
- ☐ They are an entirely objective process for assessing staff performance
- ☐ They are part of the disciplinary process

6.2 **Identify the benefits of health and safety controls from the following alternatives:**

Select ALL that apply.

- ☐ Employees breaking health and safety rules receive appropriate punishment
- ☐ The company image is protected from a poor health and safety record
- ☐ The morale of employees and others is improved
- ☐ The legal obligations for health and safety are met
- ☐ Health and safety controls save managers the job of monitoring potential safety hazards

6.3 **Which THREE of the following represent barriers to communication?**

- ☐ The choice of words provokes an emotional response
- ☐ Ensuring all elements of the communication "fit"
- ☐ The filtering out of elements that he or she does not want to deal with
- ☐ Limiting the encoding/decoding capabilities of the sender/receiver
- ☐ Physically nodding confirmation

6.4 **Which THREE of the following will influence the medium of communication that should be used in any given situation?**

- ☐ Permanency
- ☐ Necessity
- ☐ Complexity
- ☐ Severity
- ☐ Urgency

6.5 J is preparing for a meeting with her line manager at which she hopes to negotiate a pay rise. She is gathering information to support her case and assist her negotiations.

Which of the following types of information would be suitable for inclusion in her case?

Select ALL that apply.

- ☐ Published statistics relating to market pay rates.

- ☐ Examples of work she has performed to a high standard.

- ☐ Details of a client which represents significant financial benefit to J's company that was obtained as a result of J's work.

- ☐ Spreadsheet showing J's salary in comparison with others in her department. The spreadsheet was prepared for J by her friend who works in management accounts.

- ☐ A document which appears to prove the existence of a relationship between J's married manager and another colleague of J's company.

6.6 The trade union representing the workers of NickNack Company is threatening to take industrial action as a result of the decision made by the senior management to make changes to working practices without consultation.

What type of conflict does this represent?

- ☐ Horizontal
- ☐ Diagonal
- ☐ Intergroup
- ☐ Vertical

6.7 The business case for encouraging diversity in the organisation's workforce is based on the recognition that, in order to compete successfully in the global economy, discrimination in any form could mean missing out on the recruitment of the most able talent.

Successful management of diversity therefore requires that an organisation takes specific measures to enable the optimum use of its staff.

Select the THREE most important measures from the following:

☐ The setting of criteria for the selection and career advancement of all staff

☐ Supporting legislation against discrimination

☐ Encouraging flexibility in the treatment of all employees irrespective of their race, gender, age, sexual orientation, religion or political affiliation

☐ Claiming the organisation is an equal opportunity employer in its mission statement

☐ Training managers in fair appraisal methods

6.8 Fred feels that his manager Abi is picking on him for trivial things like an untidy desk and omitting to close a file drawer. Abi feels that Fred's presentation of accounts is not up to the standard expected of a qualified management accountant and has told him so. The situation in the office has deteriorated with Abi threatening disciplinary action and Fred threatening to invoke the company's grievance procedure.

Which THREE of the following would represent appropriate action by Fred and Abi respectively?

☐ Abi immediately threatening Fred with suspension

☐ Fred discussing his grievance with a staff representative

☐ Abi retracting her threat of suspension

☐ Fred threatening to report Abi to the professional body for unprofessional conduct

☐ Abi reporting the situation to her superior

6.9 **Which THREE of the following distinguish skilled negotiators from less skilled?**

☐ They spend more time asking questions

☐ They make more frequent use of counter-proposals

☐ They make many more justification claims to back up their case

☐ They spend more time checking that they understand what the other party is saying

☐ They spend more time summarising what has been said

6.10 A new head of department is into her first negotiating role with the trade union. She has been offered a great deal of advice from colleagues, including the claim that each one of the following conflict handling strategies is the most likely to yield success.

Write the appropriate conflict handling strategy against each outcome.

(i)   Accommodation
(ii)   Avoidance
(iii) Compromise
(iv)   Competition
(v)   Collaboration

Outcomes

Outcomes	Conflict handling strategies
Additional conflict will occur with damage to the organisation and to one or both parties	
A win, win situation	
Suppression of interests will result in one party losing out and difficulties may still remain	
Lack of effort to deal with causes of the conflict will mean that conflict is likely to recur	
Both parties lose out and there may be a better solution if an alternative approach was taken	

7 Control and the finance function

7.1   **Select the correct words to complete the definition of market control:**

- price mechanism
- controls
- tight
- performance measures
- competitor information

- loose
- specific
- budgets
- forecasts
- strong

Market control is the use of the [   ] and related [   ], internally and externally to control organisational behaviours. It is appropriate for use in [   ] organisational forms such as consortia and alliances.

7.2   **Select the correct words to complete the sentences below.**

- actively
- technically
- financially
- operations
- strategies
- commercial
- planning
- partners
- specific
- consultants
- gurus
- profitable

The finance function has faced pressures to become more [   ] involved in business [   ]. Many finance functions have therefore re-focused their roles as business [   ], adopting a more [   ], action orientated approach.

7.3   **The independent business partner model suggests which of the following?**

Select ALL that apply.

- ☐   The finance function should add value to the organisation
- ☐   The finance function should create value for the organisation
- ☐   The finance function should assist in the creation of strategy, ideas and opportunities
- ☐   Actual performance should be rigorously reviewed by the finance function
- ☐   The finance function should challenge any results that are better than expected

7.4 NT is a company that makes bespoke and unique hand-built furniture.

NT's reputation for outstanding pieces of furniture and high levels of customer service has strengthened over the years and demand has increased significantly. In order to continue to grow, the company is considering outsourcing some of its processes in order to generate funds to re-invest in the company in order for it to meet the higher levels of demand. NT has suggested that the following processes for potential outsourcing.

For each process advise NT as to whether the process could be outsourced, or whether it would be preferable for it to remain in-house.

(i)   Outsource
(ii)   In-house

The payroll process

Delivery of the finished products to the customer

Customer consultation and bespoke design of furniture

Build and manufacture of the furniture

IT support services

7.5 **In the context of social responsibility, what are externalities?**

☐   External costs faced by the organisation in response to social responsibility, such as compensation payments

☐   The perception of the organisation by external stakeholders

☐   The costs imposed by businesses on other people, not included in the cost of their products and activities

☐   Areas of social responsibility linked to the company, but outside its direct control, such as the business practices of a supplier

---

7.6 Organisations have a number of different options in how they position the finance function and each has its own drawbacks.

Match each of the finance structures against the description of the drawbacks below:

(i)   Finance function embedded in business area
(ii)   Shared Service Centre
(iii) Business Process Outsourcing

No sharing of knowledge and best practice

Lack the required local knowledge

Higher risk of loss of control and quality

7.7 Management control takes place at a variety of levels including the strategic, tactical and operational levels.

J Company is currently reviewing its control systems and you are required to advise the project team on the appropriate level at which each of the following aspects of control should be set.

Match each of the control aspects listed below to the appropriate level in the control hierarchy.

(i)   Setting and reviewing the organisational structure
(ii)   Computerisation of inventory control
(iii) Setting of the production budget

Level in control hierarchy	Aspects of control
Strategic	
Tactical	
Operational	

7.8 You have been asked to advise on the most appropriate form of control in the various departments of manufacturing Company A.

The manufacturing department involves the assembly and packing of toy cars. Employees are paid a basic salary plus a bonus based on the number of cars produced minus an amount for any rejects.

Employees in the wages department attend to all payroll related tasks and provide management with the necessary information for control of operations.

The finance department is staffed by professional accountants.

Indicate which of the four forms of management control is appropriate for which department by writing the appropriate form of control into the correct departmental box.

(i)   Bureaucratic
(ii)   Personal
(iii)   Output
(iv)   Clan

Departments	Manufacturing	Wages	Finance
Management Control Type			

7.9 **Which of the following is not a role of a mentor?**

☐   Guidance in tackling projects
☐   Day-to-day management of protégées
☐   Acting as a role model
☐   Advice in drawing up personal development plans

7.10 The CIMA Code of Ethics contains five fundamental principles.

Match each principle to its description.

(i)   Confidentiality
(ii)   Integrity
(iii)   Professional behaviour
(iv)   Professional competence and due care
(v)   Objectivity

A professional accountant should be straightforward and honest in all professional and business relationships

A professional accountant should not allow bias, conflict of interest or undue influence of others to override professional or business judgments

A professional accountant has a continuing duty to maintain professional knowledge and skill and should act diligently and in accordance with applicable technical and professional standards when providing professional services

A professional accountant should not disclose any information acquired as a result of professional and business relationships without proper and specific authority unless there is a legal or professional right or duty to disclose

A professional accountant should comply with relevant laws and regulations, and should avoid any action that discredits the profession

8 Change management

8.1 **If the nature of the change is incremental and the scope of the change is realignment, what type of change is occurring?**

☐ Evolution
☐ Adaptation
☐ Reconstruction
☐ Revolution

8.2 Kotter and Schlesinger's contingency approach to change identified a number of change management strategies along with the contexts within which they could be most successfully applied.

Match each change strategy with its favourable context using the words below.

Favourable contexts where	Change strategies
There is a lack of information/analysis	☐
Initiators lack information to change & others have power to resist	☐
People resist because of adjustment problems	☐
Someone or some group will lose out and where that group has power to resist	☐
Other facilities fail or are too expensive	☐
Speed is essential & initiators have high power	☐

(a) Explicit and implicit coercion
(b) Manipulation and co-option
(c) Participation and Involvement
(d) Facilitation and support
(e) Negotiation and agreement
(f) Education and communication

8.3 **Which of the following THREE items engender resistance to change?**

☐ Downward adjustment to symbols of status such as a company car
☐ Opportunities for participation
☐ Questioning of an individual's frame of reference
☐ Raising concerns for security
☐ Directive management style used in a hierarchical power structure

8.4 **Select THREE items from the following list which represent internal triggers for change in a company.**

☐ Ageing of the company's infrastructure
☐ Sudden drop in the company's market share
☐ A new Chief Executive Officer begins work
☐ Industrial action by the workforce
☐ Shift in exchange rates in which company goods are traded

8.5 Which of the statements below are forces for change and which are forces against change?

Select the correct option for each of the phrases below.

(i)   Force for change
(ii)   Force against

Commitment of employees to the change	

Bureaucracy	

Clear articulation of a vision for the future	

Traditional ways of working	

Command and control management style	

Encouragement and support from the top	

8.6 CT Company is embarking on a programme of change which it intends to be evolutionary.

Write the words or phrases to show the nature of change and the scope of change for CT Company.

(i)   Transformation
(ii)   Big bang
(iii)   Realignment
(iv)   Incremental

The nature of change will be: [   ]

The scope of change will be: [   ]

8.7 In the context of change management, which of the following best describes the role of an organisations strategic leadership?

☐ To challenge things that are taken for granted
☐ To implement the change
☐ Translation of the overall change strategy into forms suited to specific local contexts
☐ To get others to follow the change willingly
☐ To bring a fresh point of view and break down the constraints of the existing paradigm

8.8 In the context of change which of the following describes a paradigm?

☐ Entrenched assumptions and habits of mind.
☐ Habitual behaviours that members of the organisation display both internally and externally.
☐ Visible things which can be used as levers of change.

8.9 Which of the following maybe a reason for resistance to a change programme?

Select ALL that apply.

☐ High levels of uncertainty
☐ Increase in workload
☐ Sense of embarrassment
☐ Rapid change
☐ Loss of autonomy
☐ Lack skills and competence

8.10 When a business is in terminal decline and faces closure or takeover, there is a need for rapid and extensive change in order to achieve cost reduction and revenue generation. This is a turnaround strategy. Johnson, Scholes & Whittington identify seven elements of such a strategy.

Which THREE of the following are elements of the turnaround strategy?

☐ Consistent financial structure
☐ Attention to target markets
☐ Maintaining the same management team
☐ Communication with stakeholders
☐ Crisis stabilisation

9 Introduction to project management

9.1 Libby is the project manager for an IT project which has the objective of improving the functionality of the company's website. This will involve designing a system which enhances the customer experience of navigating the website and simplifies the process for placing orders for the company's products - which are stationery items (paper clips, rulers etc) shaped like animals. The launch of the new website is time critical; customers need their tortoise-shaped drawing pins.

The project must be completed in three months' time but is experiencing significant slippage and is behind schedule. Which of the following things should Libby do to get back on track?

☐ Maintain quality and reduce resources
☐ Increase resources and increase quality
☐ Reduce resources and increase quality
☐ Increase resources and maintain quality

9.2 **According to PRINCE2 methodology, which process ensures that all planned deliverables are completed as required?**

☐ Initiation
☐ Managing product delivery
☐ Managing stage boundaries
☐ Project assurance

9.3 **Calculate the float time for a project activity if the earliest start time is day 5, the latest finish time is day 22, and the total time needed for the work is 14 days.**

Give your answer to the nearest whole day.

☐☐☐☐☐☐ day/s

9.4 Bethan, a project manager, has identified a number of risks associated with her new project to open up a Cat Hotel. One of the risks has a high likelihood of happening, but will have a low impact on the project.

Which risk management strategy should be used here?

☐ Transfer
☐ Avoid
☐ Reduce
☐ Accept

9.5 **Select the stage in the project lifecycle that matches the activity.**

(i) Initiation
(ii) Planning
(iii) Execution
(iv) Project closure

Project feasibility

Testing

Identifying project risk

Audit of deliverables

Setting milestones and control gates

Specifying project scope

Cost breakdown structure

Exception reporting

9.6 **Which of the following can be used to manage project uncertainty, with specific reference to time?**

Select all that apply.

☐ PERT
☐ Financial feasibility
☐ Buffering
☐ Scenario planning
☐ SWOT
☐ Economic feasibility
☐ Work breakdown structure

9.7 RCT Company has initiated a project with the objective of building a new manufacturing plant for its washing detergent products, soaps, and chemical cleaners. The plant will need to install manufacturing processes and equipment which will enable easy switching of production between the different product lines. It will also need to assess how the waste from the manufacturing process is disposed of safety.

Match the types of feasibility with the questions.

Types of feasibility can be used more than once.

(i) Social feasibility
(ii) Economic feasibility
(iii) Ecological feasibility
(iv) Technical feasibility

How will waste products be disposed of safely?

How much disruption will the building of the plant cause?

What is the likelihood of the local community objecting to the project?

Are the manufacturing processes and equipment available?

What pollution could be caused by the project?

What is included in the costs of the project?

9.8 The earliest event time (EET) and latest event time (LET) of the final node on the network analysis will be the same.

Is this statement True or False?

☐ True
☐ False

9.9 **Match the project planning technique against the relevant description of its purpose.**

(i) incorporates risk by adding in slack into risky activities
(ii) is used to analyse the interrelationship between project tasks
(iii) are a graphical representation of project activities
(iv) assists with risk in project time planning

Network Analysis ☐

Buffering ☐

PERT ☐

Gantt Charts ☐

9.10 **What is the duration of the critical path for this project?**

A company is about to undertake a project about which the following data is available.

Activity	Preceded by activity	Duration (Days)
A	–	3
B	–	5
C	B	2
D	A	1
E	A	6
F	D	3
G	C,E	3

Duration of critical path is ☐

---

10 The project team

10.1 **According to Tuckman, at what stage of the process of group formation is it when members begin to set agreed standards and allocate roles?**

☐ Storming
☐ Forming
☐ Norming
☐ Performing

10.2 FOPSSound is a well established group of music producers, with members working well together for 4 years. However, one of the team is branching out on his own and another has decided that he needs to spend more time with his family, so is retiring. Two new members of staff have been recruited to replace them.

What stage of team development will the group need to revert to in order that team cohesiveness is restored?

☐ Storming
☐ Norming
☐ Forming
☐ Performing

10.3 Although there are numerous benefits of working as a team, there can be some negative effects too.

Which of the following are the negative effects of team working?

Select ALL that apply.

☐ The Abilene Paradox
☐ Synergy
☐ Group think
☐ Problem solving
☐ Conformity
☐ Role ambiguity
☐ Creativity

10.4 **What is the MAIN difference between a 'group' and a 'team'?**

☐ A team has an identity, a group does not
☐ A team has a mix of personalities, a group does not
☐ A team has a common purpose, a group does not
☐ A team has commitment, a group does not

10.5 **What is the role of the project sponsor?**

☐ Provides and is accountable for the resources invested in the project
☐ Communicates the project vision within the organisation
☐ Takes responsibility for delivering the project on time
☐ Represents the interests of the project board

10.6 Mr Squirrel has built a new team to work on a project. He has evaluated the group according to Belbin's team roles and has identified that the group is unbalanced. The group is missing a number of important roles necessary to be effective. Mr Squirrel needs someone to control and organise the group's activities, and there is no one who is chasing and ensuring deadlines are met. The group is also missing someone to support other team members and diffuse potential conflict situations.

Match the team role to the description given.

(i) Plant
(ii) Co-ordinator
(iii) Shaper
(iv) Monitor Evaluator
(v) Completer/Finisher
(vi) Implementer
(vii) Team Worker
(viii) Resource Investigator

Someone to control and organise the group's activities

Someone to chase and ensure deadlines are met

Someone to support other team members and diffuse potential conflict situations

10.7   To be successful in the management of change, a project manager will:

Select THREE options.

☐   Adopt an appropriate leadership style for managing change
☐   Understand the overall strategic objectives of the project
☐   Make use of formal means only to communicate with project team members
☐   Be sensitive to the environmental and organisational contexts of the change
☐   Drive change entirely from the top

10.8   **Which of the following are roles of the project manager?**

Select ALL that apply.

☐   Coordinates project activities
☐   Approves the project plan
☐   Provides resources
☐   Provides leadership for the project team
☐   Responsible for successful delivery of project objectives
☐   Initiates the project

10.9   **Which of the following is a potential problem with individual performance-related pay (PRP) as a motivator?**

☐   Its effect on organisational communication
☐   Its relevance to business objectives
☐   The fact that it does not relate to individuals' wage or salary grades
☐   Its effect on project team motivation

10.10 Grant is a member of a project team. His colleagues in the team rely on him to read and check complex project documentation.

Grant has a keen eye for detail and often identifies minor details in documents that others miss but may be of significance.

Despite the diligent approach, Grant always meets his deadlines.

However, some of Grant's colleagues feel frustrated when he refuses to involve others.

He can hold up progress as he will not agree to the team signing off project documents until all of his concerns are fully discussed.

According to Belbin's team roles theory, Grant is an example of which of the following?

☐   Implementer
☐   Completer – finisher
☐   Monitor – evaluator
☐   Shaper
☐   Plant
☐   Resource Investigator

11 Mixed Bank 1

11.1   **Match each aspect of a position audit with its definition:**

(i)   Corporate appraisal
(ii)   Opportunities
(iii)   Weaknesses
(iv)   Environmental analysis
(v)   Strengths
(vi)   Threats

The combination of the internal position audit and the external analysis to produce a SWOT analysis.

Internal failures that hinder the organisation from meeting its goals

Events or changes in the organisation's environment which are unfavourable to the organisation and need to be guarded against

Events or changes outside the organisation that could be exploited to the organisation's benefit.

11.2   **When analysing a company's opportunities and threats which of the following would you ignore?**

☐   Changes in customer tastes
☐   Market share
☐   Competitor response to a successful marketing campaign
☐   View of the political party in power

11.3   Various sales teams within LEO plc are monitored on the volume and value of their sales. Their relative performance is compared on a monthly basis with the intention of ascertaining best practice.

This is an example of which of the following exercises?

☐   Competitive benchmarking
☐   Internal benchmarking
☐   Reverse engineering
☐   Functional benchmarking
☐   Operational benchmarking

11.4   **Which of the following statements about Organic organisations are true?**

Select ALL that apply.

☐   An organisation exists even before it is filled with people.
☐   Pay scales are prescribed according to the position or office held in the organisation structure.
☐   Procedures ensure that, regardless of who carries out tasks, they should be executed in the same way.
☐   There are differences of status, determined by people's greater expertise and experience.
☐   The degree of commitment employees have to the goals of the firm and the team is more extensive.
☐   Corporate culture is a powerful guide to behaviour.

11.5 Research has indicated that workers in country A display characteristics such as toughness and the desire for material wealth and possessions, while workers in country B value personal relationships, belonging and the quality of life.

According to Hofstede's theory, these distinctions relate to which of the following cultural dimensions?

- ☐ Power – distance
- ☐ Individualism – collectivism
- ☐ Masculinity – femininity
- ☐ Uncertainty avoidance

11.6 There are many reasons why a message may not be communicated effectively.

For each of the situations below, identify the likely barrier which may prevent effective communication from occurring:

- (i) Noise
- (ii) Overload
- (iii) Cultural Values
- (iv) Jargon
- (v) Priorities
- (vi) Selective reporting
- (vii) Timing
- (viii) Distortion

A phone conversation with a client is interrupted as a result of interference on the line.

```
┌─────────────────┐
│                 │
└─────────────────┘
```

Information relating to an organisational restructure is provided on a strictly 'need to know' basis.

```
┌─────────────────┐
│                 │
└─────────────────┘
```

The new CEO determines that email will now be used as the primary method of communication to ensure documentary evidence is in place should it be needed. This rule is to be applied to all messages from daily updates, to social events, to key operational messages.

```
┌─────────────────┐
│                 │
└─────────────────┘
```

11.7 Performance targets related to pricing would be best considered under which perspective of the balanced scorecard?

- ☐ Customer
- ☐ Internal business
- ☐ Innovation and learning
- ☐ Financial

11.8 Association with respected and influential stakeholders can enhance the personal status and thus the power base of the change agent. Similarly, association with a high status change agent can assist more junior managers to overcome resistance to change.

Which of the political mechanisms used to exert influence by change managers is being described here?

- ☐ Political mechanisms
- ☐ Manipulation of resources
- ☐ Elites relationships
- ☐ Exploitation of subsystems
- ☐ Symbolic activity

11.9 **Calculate the overall expected duration of the project:**

Activity	Preceding activity	Activity duration in weeks
A	-	8
B	-	10
C	-	6
D	A	8
E	B, C	9
F	C	14
G	D, E	14
H	F, G	6

The overall expected duration of the project is [   ] weeks.

11.10 A team is winding up a challenging project that it has been working on for some time. Next week, the same team will go on to a new project with quite different challenges.

Which stage of the group development model is this team likely to be going through?

☐ Norming
☐ Dorming
☐ Adjourning
☐ Performing

12 Mixed Bank 2

12.1 **Complete the paragraph using the words available.**

Available options:

- inside-out view
- outside-in
- positioning
- resource-based
- unique

The [   ] view sees competitive advantage as coming from the way a firm positions itself in relation to its competitors, customers and stakeholders. The [   ] view suggests that the organisation should focus on developing a [   ] competence or asset and then find a market which wants it. This is also referred to as an [   ].

12.2 A motor vehicle manufacturer monitors its international political environment and the directors have come to the conclusion that regulations relating to carbon dioxide emissions will be relaxed in the next twelve months or so. However, the company is to pursue a programme of lobbying international governments in order to maintain current regulations. The manufacturer considers its ability to meet the current standards as a source of competitive advantage.

Which of the following best describes the manufacturer's plans to lobby the governments?

☐ Protectionism
☐ Economic liberalisation
☐ Buffering
☐ Bridging

12.3 HSOP Ltd operates a history museum targeted at families with children. Its exhibits are fun and interactive and are often accompanied by performances from its staff. LORE Ltd operates a zoo in the same city as HSOP's museum. It is targeted at the entertainment of families but is seen as more educational than fun.

What level of competitor does this represent?

- ☐ Generic
- ☐ Form
- ☐ Industry
- ☐ Brand

12.4 In her interview Mary has been told her role involves tasks that are specific to the firm and require firm-specific skills and experience. She will need to be functionally flexible in terms of multi-skilling and even re-skilling, though training will be provided for this.

This type of worker is referred to as:

- ☐ Core group
- ☐ Peripheral group
- ☐ Flexible labour
- ☐ Contractual fringe

12.5 **Which of Deal and Kennedy's corporate cultures is Bow-wing, an aircraft manufacturer, likely to have?**

- ☐ Process culture
- ☐ Bet your company culture
- ☐ Hard macho culture
- ☐ Work hard play hard culture

12.6 **Match the most appropriate method of communication for each of the following situations:**

- (i) Email
- (ii) Brainstorming session
- (iii) One-to-one meeting
- (iv) Team meeting
- (v) Large scale meeting

A general update on the achievements of the company needs to be communicated to all staff [   ]

A product is going to be re-launched and ideas for the marketing campaign need to be generated [   ]

The payroll manager has become aware of a time-keeping problem with one of the payroll clerks [   ]

The organisation is planning a major restructure and the initial plans need to be announced [   ]

The sales team require an update on their achievements against targets for the last quarter [   ]

12.7 Large companies often include a reference to social responsibility in their mission statements.

Which THREE of the aspirations below reflect a genuine concern for socially responsible behaviour?

To keep employees informed of policy, progress and problems.

To provide good working conditions and decent rewards for all employees.

To support the local community and preserve the environment.

To conform with legislation in reducing the harmful waste products from our processes to an acceptable level.

To pay at least the minimum wage to all employees.

12.8 The decision to introduce a home delivery service may be part of a long-term plan to close down all of the BAMM stores over a number of years with a view of becoming an online retailer only. Such a change would lead to a change in the organisation's culture and business model.

Which type of change is BAMM experiencing?

☐ Adaptation
☐ Reconstruction
☐ Evolution
☐ Revolution

12.9 What is the duration of the critical path for this project?

Activity	Immediately preceding activity	Duration (weeks)
A	-	5
B	-	4
C	A	2
D	B	1
E	B	5
F	B	5
G	C, D	4
H	F	3
I	F	2

☐ weeks are needed for the critical path.

12.10 Team-member Tom is one of those people who is dynamic and thrives on pressure. He tends to be the one who challenges and pushes other team members, sometimes annoying or upsetting them - but also getting the team past difficult periods.

Which of Belbin's team roles does Tom exercise?

☐ Plant
☐ Co-ordinator (chair)
☐ Implementer
☐ Shaper
☐ Monitor-evaluator
☐ Completer-finisher

13 Mixed Bank 3

13.1   In order for a strength to have real benefit to a business it has to be linked to critical success factors.

What are critical success factors?

☐   Factors fundamental to strategic success.
☐   Factors contributing to strategic success.
☐   Factors necessary to match strengths to opportunities.
☐   Factors necessary to build on strengths.

13.2   **When determining a nation's comparative advantage, the consideration of the country's culture and management style relates to which part of Porter's Diamond?**

☐   Factor conditions
☐   Related and supporting industries
☐   Firm strategy, structure and rivalry
☐   Demand conditions

13.3   **In the context of Mendelow's matrix which stakeholders should be 'kept informed'.**

☐   High interest, high power
☐   High interest, low power
☐   Low interest, high power
☐   Low interest, low power

13.4   **According to Handy's Shamrock organisation write the employee group against its description below:**

(i)   Employee group
(ii)   Contractual fringe
(iii)   Professional core
(iv)   Flexible labour

Permanently-employed people who represent the distinctive knowledge and competences of the firm. They are qualified professionals, technicians and managers. Their commitment is focused on their work and career within the organisation.

Temporary and part-time workers who can be brought in as and when needed, especially to meet peaks in the demand for services. They are crucial in maintaining standards of service, so it is important for the firm not to treat them 'casually'.

External providers who are able to undertake non-core activities or provide specialist services, more economically than the firm could manage internally.

13.5   **Which of Deal and Kennedy's corporate cultures would you be likely to find at Pewlett-Hackard, a computer manufacturer?**

☐   Process culture
☐   Bet your company culture
☐   Hard macho culture
☐   Work hard play hard culture

13.6 **Are the following statements true or false?**

Distributive bargaining is an approach to negotiation concerned with joint problem solving.

Conflict resolution aims to reduce resentment and preserve relationships by allowing both parties to obtain all of their desired outcomes.

Negotiation is a process whereby two parties come together to confer, with a view to concluding a jointly acceptable agreement.

13.7 D is a CIMA student working towards full CIMA membership. He works in the accounts department of B company. D's manager, F, has asked D to process an expense claim for dinner and hotel expenses from the previous night. As D has access to F's calendar, he knows that F had a personal, not work related, engagement that night.

Which threat is D facing?

☐ Advocacy threat
☐ Familiarity threat
☐ Intimidation threat
☐ Self-interest threat

13.8 Wholesome supermarkets recently introduced a home delivery service to customers in the London area. The company is attempting to move with the times as competing supermarkets already offer this service. There are no plans to close any of its supermarkets.

Which type of change is Wholesome experiencing?

☐ Adaptation
☐ Reconstruction
☐ Evolution
☐ Revolution

13.9 **Which of the following project stakeholders is the person who provides the resources for a project?**

☐ Project sponsor
☐ Project manager
☐ Project owner
☐ Project customer

13.10 Team-leader Arnica has given a team briefing stating the current situation and asking for suggestions to move the project on.

What stage is the team current at?

☐ Forming
☐ Storming
☐ Norming
☐ Performing

14 Mixed Bank 4

14.1 **In the context of Mendelow's stakeholder matrix which of the following are likely to increase the following stakeholders' levels of power.**

Select ALL that apply.

☐ Trade union's membership increases amongst the employees of an organisation

☐ The IT department recruits more IT specialists to accommodate a company's decision to sell all its products online

☐ A shareholder group meet to discuss a proposal from the directors

☐ A supplier wins a contract to be sole supplier of one of the company's competitors

☐ A department's budget has been reduced by 50%

14.2 **Complete the following paragraph using the available words below:**

- quotas
- tariffs
- taxes
- subsidies
- protectionist
- free trade
- buffering

The government in the country of Utopica has recently introduced import [＿＿＿＿＿＿＿＿＿＿] which limit the volume of overseas meat that can be brought into Utopica. They have also made [＿＿＿＿＿＿＿＿＿＿] available to domestic meat producers in order to increase the amount of meat produced within the country.

This is an example of a [＿＿＿＿＿＿＿＿＿] policy.

14.3 **In the context of stakeholder analysis and Mendelow's matrix, which of the following axes are used to assess the position of a stakeholder?**

Select ALL that apply.

☐ Level of interest
☐ Level of knowledge
☐ Level of power
☐ Level within the hierarchy
☐ Legitimacy

14.4 **Companies and departments can follow different organisational forms. Write the organisational form against the department to which it applies.**

(i) Organic organisational form
(ii) Mechanistic organisational form

The payroll department of a firm has well-defined tasks such as paying salaries at the end of the month. There is little variation. Controls are needed to ensure processing accuracy and to avoid fraud.   [＿＿＿＿＿＿＿＿]

The 'creative department' of an advertising agency, employs a number of professional experts such as copywriters, graphic designers and account executives, who work on projects.   [＿＿＿＿＿＿＿＿]

14.5 **Write the elements of the cultural web beside the description to which it applies.**

  (i)   Power structures
  (ii)   Stories
  (iii) The paradigm
  (iv)   Control systems
  (v)   Symbols
  (vi)   Organisational structures
  (vii) Rituals and routines

The guiding set of beliefs, values and assumptions that shape how the organisation sees itself and its purpose.	
The 'mythology' of the organisation: tales of successes and failures, how things got to be the way they are.	
Symbolic behaviours such as business formulation and ceremonies, as well as formal procedures and customs.	
Ways in which control is exercised via standards, monitoring and supervision.	

14.6 K has made the following decisions in preparing for a negotiation meeting with a potential client.

Match the decisions she has made to the relevant key elements of preparing for negotiations.

  (i)   Personalities
  (ii)   Purpose
  (iii) Pace
  (iv)   Plan

After numerous discussions with the potential client, K is intending to secure a deal with the client at this meeting.	
The potential client has a reputation for being a fierce negotiator and driving hard bargains.	
As numerous discussions have already been held, few introductions will be required.	
A break-out room will be required for discussions between K and her team at various intervals.	

14.7 **Select the correct words to complete the sentences below:**

  - non-executive
  - executive
  - management
  - organisation
  - independent
  - employees
  - numerous
  - directors

  - review
  - prepare
  - auditors
  - qualified accountants
  - several
  - carry out
  - over-see

Companies should have an audit committee consisting of [   ] directors, the majority of whom should be [   ]. The audit committee should [   ] the audit, and the independence and objectivity of the [   ].

14.8 Change initiatives can be used for unintended purposes; for example, improved technology provided to improve performance may be used simply to cut staffing levels, defeating the overall objective.

Which unintended outcome of a change programme is being described here?

☐ Ritualisation of change.
☐ Hijacked process of change.
☐ Erosion.
☐ Reinvention.

14.9 Projects present some management challenges.

Which of the following are potential challenges for project managers?

Select ALL that apply.

☐ Teambuilding
☐ Expected problems
☐ Unexpected problems
☐ Delayed benefit
☐ Potential for conflict

14.10 **Which of the following principles of classical management is challenged by matrix management?**

☐ Structuring the organisation on functional lines
☐ Structuring the organisation on geographical lines
☐ Unity of command
☐ Decentralisation of decision-making

15 Mixed Bank 5

15.1 **Which of the following are examples of strategic alliances?**

Select ALL that apply.

☐ Franchising
☐ Acquisitions
☐ Joint ventures
☐ Mergers
☐ Consortia
☐ Licensing

15.2 **In a LoNGPEST analysis which of the following are recognised sections of the analysis?**

Select all that apply.

☐ Long-term
☐ National
☐ Governmental
☐ Technological
☐ Global
☐ Natural
☐ Tax

15.3 In the context of the Boston Consulting Group matrix what do cash cows and dogs have in common?

- ☐ High relative market share
- ☐ High market growth
- ☐ Low relative market share
- ☐ Low market growth

15.4 Rensis Likert (New Patterns of Management) described a range of four management styles or 'systems'.

Write the management style beside the management behaviour to which it applies:

- (i) Participative
- (ii) Exploitative authoritative
- (iii) Benevolent authoritative
- (iv) Consultative

The leader has only superficial trust in subordinates, motivates by reward and, though sometimes involving others in problem solving, is basically paternalistic.

The leader imposes decisions, never delegates, motives by threat, has little communication with subordinates and does not encourage teamwork.

The leader has confidence in subordinates, who are allowed to make decisions for themselves. Motivation is by reward for achieving goals set by participation, and there is a substantial amount of sharing of ideas, opinions and co-operation.

The leader listens to subordinates but controls decision making, motivates by a level of involvement, and will use the ideas and suggestions of subordinates constructively.

15.5 Harrison classified four types of culture.

Write the type of culture beside the description to which it applies.

- (i) Person
- (ii) Task
- (iii) Role
- (iv) Power

Culture is shaped by one individual

Culture is a bureaucratic culture shaped by rationality, rules and procedures

Culture is shaped by a focus on outputs and results

Culture is shaped by the interests of individuals

15.6 Which of the following are characteristics of successful negotiators as identified by John Hunt?

Select ALL that apply.

- ☐ They directly confront the opposition
- ☐ They consider a wide range of options
- ☐ They respond immediately with counter proposals
- ☐ They use emollient verbal techniques: 'would it be helpful if we...?'
- ☐ They summarise on behalf of all involved
- ☐ They advance single arguments insistently and avoid long winded, multiple reason arguments

15.7 The arguments for and against social responsibility are complex

The traditional approach to social responsibility can best be summed up by which of the following?

- ☐ Organisations exist for the benefits of shareholders
- ☐ Organisations are political systems
- ☐ Organisations exist for the benefit of all stakeholders
- ☐ Organisations are social arrangements

15.8 Staff are likely to become confused and demotivated if practical adjustments, e.g. to systems, do not fit well with the overall intent of the change programme.

Which unintended outcome of a change programme is being described here?

- ☐ Ivory tower change
- ☐ Lack of attention to symbols
- ☐ Behavioural compliance
- ☐ Uncontrolled efforts

15.9 **Which ONE of the following provides a common understanding of a project for all its stakeholders by defining the project's overall boundaries?**

- ☐ Project lifecycle
- ☐ Project milestones
- ☐ Project scope
- ☐ Project schedule

15.10 **Which of the following is not an advantage of a matrix structure?**

- ☐ Dual authority
- ☐ Greater flexibility
- ☐ Employee motivation
- ☐ Improved communications

16 Mixed Bank 6

16.1 Company HJJ is considering whether it should continue its payroll administration in-house or outsource it.

Complete the sentences below using the available words below:

- specificity
- hierarchy
- transaction
- market
- temporal

If Company HJJ decides to do its payroll in-house, managers will then focus on monitoring and controlling

that function's use and performance. This is known as a [   ] solution. The company may enter into a contract to buy in the payroll services from an external supplier as long as the

[   ] costs associated with this last option are not too high. This option is called the

[   ] solution.

16.2 **In the context of Porter's 5 Forces which one of the following definitions best describes a substitute product or service?**

☐   One that meets similar needs and is manufactured in the same way
☐   One that meets different needs but is made or delivered in the same way
☐   One that meets the same needs but is made or delivered in a different way
☐   One that meets different needs at the same time

16.3 **Which of the following are examples of formal collection of data from outside sources?**

Select ALL that apply.

☐   Market research to ascertain customers' buying attitudes

☐   Hiring a consultant in order to train employees on new health and safety legislation

☐   Analysis of the sales ledger to identify customers with a good payment history

☐   Observation of established work patterns by an IT specialist in order to design a new information system

☐   Television news report about a competitor's actions seen by the chief executive's husband

16.4 D I WHY? hardware store recently placed an advertisement for new shop floor staff. Having selected a number of candidates to attend an interview, Joe-Boy the HR Manager advises Jessie-May, the departmental manager, of company policy regarding approved interviewing methods. The final decision on which candidate to recruit remains with the respective department manager.

What kind of authority does Joe-Boy have?

☐   Line authority
☐   Staff authority
☐   Functional authority
☐   Departmental authority

16.5 **Which type of culture according to Harrison's cultural models would best fit with a matrix structure?**

☐   Person
☐   Role
☐   Power
☐   Task

16.6 **Which TWO of the below are the main elements involved in negotiation?**

☐   Purposeful persuasion
☐   Constructive compromise
☐   Conflict resolution
☐   Problem solving
☐   Distributive bargaining
☐   Integrative bargaining

16.7 T has been newly appointed in the management accounts function at Q company.

T's first job is to meet with staff from various departments to discuss budgets and prepare revised forecasts.

T is unsure about the structure of the organisation and the responsibilities of the various staff within the departments.

T is therefore unsure where to start or who he should be speaking to.

Who would be best placed to advise T in relation to these concerns?

☐ T's line manager
☐ The Finance Director
☐ T's mentor
☐ T's junior assistant

16.8 **Match the type of change to the description to which it applies.**

(i)   Adaptation
(ii)   Reconstruction
(iii) Evolution
(iv)   Revolution

A change which is a rapid and wide-ranging response to extreme pressures for change. A long period of strategic drift may lead to a crisis that can only be dealt with in this way. It will be very obvious and is likely to affect most aspects of both what the organisation does and how it does them. ⬛

A change undertaken within an existing paradigm, but requiring rapid and extensive action. It is a common response to a long-term decline in performance. ⬛

The most common type of change. It does not require the development of a new paradigm and proceeds step by step. ⬛

A change which is an incremental process that leads to a new paradigm. It may arise from careful analysis and planning or may be the result of learning processes. Its transformational nature may not be obvious while it is taking place. ⬛

16.9 **Which ONE of the following is the term used in project management to assess how achievable various project options are?**

☐ Feasibility analysis
☐ Risk analysis
☐ Contingency analysis
☐ Resource analysis

16.10 A large supermarket chain has purchased land for a new out-of-town shopping development in an area of recognised natural beauty. The organisation is now preparing plans for infrastructure development (road access, parking, power) and construction.

Using Mendelow's power/interest matrix what strategy would the organisation use for the local nature appreciation groups?

☐ Consult and involve
☐ Keep informed
☐ Keep satisfied
☐ Minimal effort

17 Mixed Bank 7

17.1 Company A has recently entered into an agreement with Company Z to manufacture and distribute company Z's products under Company Z's brand name.

Company B has a small head office in Newtown. All workers work from home using information technology as an enabler for communication and collaboration. Most workers do not have employment contracts with company B.

Company C was set up as a temporary measure by Companies D, E and F. Its objective is to perform some confidential research and development work.

Match the companies with the type of organisational structure.

(i)   Consortium
(ii)   Franchise
(ii)   Virtual network

Company A   [   ]

Company B   [   ]

Company C   [   ]

17.2 **Which one of the following definitions best describes a government's macroeconomic policy of import-substitution?**

☐   The government reduces import taxes and tariffs to make imports more attractive in the domestic market and removes the country's dependence on expensive imports

☐   The government reduces import taxes and tariffs to make exports more attractive in the domestic market and thus removes the country's dependence on expensive imports

☐   The government uses import taxes and tariffs to protect developing industries and reduce the country's dependence on foreign imports

☐   The government uses import taxes and tariffs to fund the development of new substitute products and services in order to remove the country's dependence on foreign imports.

17.3 **Which of the following are potential advantages of a focus strategy?**

Select ALL that apply.

☐   Economies of scale are reduced.
☐   The needs of the segment may eventually become less distinct from the main market.
☐   Competitors can move into the segment with increased resources.
☐   Niche market segments can be more secure.
☐   The firm does not try to achieve too much with too little early in the business cycle.

17.4   **Write the appropriate words beside the description to which it applies:**

Descriptions:

(i)   Accountability
(ii)   Authority
(iii)   Delegation
(iv)   Empowerment power
(v)   Influence
(vi)   Responsibility

The process by which one person modifies the behaviour or attitude of another.
[   ]

The term for making workers (and particularly work teams) responsible for achieving, and even setting, work targets, with the freedom to make decisions about how they are to be achieved.
[   ]

The right to do something, or to ask someone else to do it and expect it to be done.
[   ]

17.5   You have just read Charles Handy's Gods of Management and you want to see whether you have understood what Handy was getting at.

Match the god to the organisational description.

(i)   Athena
(ii)   Zeus
(iii)   Dionysus
(iv)   Apollo

The purpose of the organisation is to serve the interests of the individuals who make it up. Management is directed at facilitating and administering.
[   ]

The organisation is controlled by a key central figure, owner or founder. Power is direct, personal and informal. Suits small organisations where people get on well.
[   ]

Management is directed at outputs, problems solved and projects completed. Team-based, horizontally-structured, flexible and valuing expertise – to get the job done.
[   ]

Classical, rational organisation with bureaucracy. Stable, slow-changing, formalised and impersonal. Authority based on position and function.
[   ]

17.6   There are five strategies for resolving conflict.

Write the correct labels into the boxes in the diagram using the list of words below.

(i)   Forcing/competing
(ii)   Collaborating
(iii)   Compromising
(iv)   Avoiding
(v)   Accomodating

17.7   **The following responsibilities are imposed on employers as a result of the Management of Health and Safety at Work Regulations 1992.**

True or false?

To carry out risk assessments, generally in writing, of all work hazards at least once

To introduce controls to prevent risks

To identify employees who are especially at risk

To provide information to employees about health and safety

17.8   **Which of the following are aspects of the context of change as proposed by Balogun and Hope Hailey?**

Select ALL that apply.

☐   Scope of change
☐   Preservation required
☐   Facilitation provided
☐   Diversity of experience
☐   Capacity to undertake
☐   Driving forces
☐   Readiness of workforce
☐   Power to effect
☐   Participation allowed

17.9 **At what stage in the project lifecycle is the scope of a project determined?**

- ☐ Planning
- ☐ Initiation
- ☐ Growth
- ☐ Control

17.10 A company has established a project team to design a new information system.

The team has had a few meetings to discuss how they are going to tackle the work, and who would do what, but some early ideas have been unsuccessful.

Group members are still putting forward a number of very innovative ideas, but they often disagree strongly with each other.

The group members appear to be dividing into two 'camps' each of which has an unofficial 'leader'.

These two individuals agree about very little and appear to dislike each other.

According to Tuckman, which stage in group development has the project team reached?

- ☐ Norming
- ☐ Performing
- ☐ Storming
- ☐ Dorming
- ☐ Forming

18 Mixed Bank 8

18.1 Transaction cost analysis recognises that a business carries out a series of transactions.

Which of the following is not a transaction cost associated with outsourcing the work of the payroll department?

- ☐ Loss of internal skills
- ☐ Contract price
- ☐ Contract negotiation costs
- ☐ Performance monitoring costs

18.2 **GHI Corp has decided to engage in some corporate political activity but they don't know how to refer to these activities. Match the activity to the definition.**

Activity options:

- • Buffering
- • Bridging

Definitions

1 Reading newspapers and watching news bulletins, consulting with their legal team, and attending forums. All in order to ensure they are aware of any changes in political direction which may affect them and can respond to them. ⬚

2 Taking their local MP out to lunch and campaigning the Department for Business, Innovation & Skills in order to try to persuade the government not to implement a particular bit of legislation that will impact them negatively. ⬚

18.3 **Determine whether the following statements are true or false.**

In the context of the Boston Consulting Group matrix relative market share is assessed as a ratio. It is the market share of one company compared to the market share of the largest competitor providing that same product.

☐

Exploitation of the learning curve in early stages of production of a new product may help in the pursuit of a cost leadership strategy.

☐

Where one organisation sells home improvements and another sells package holidays these organisations may be described as form competitors.

☐

18.4 Stevie Jobbs (Head of HR at Stor-less supermarkets) has observed that different managers across the company's operations adopt very different attitudes to attending corporate meetings. She has recently noted a number of comments made by different managers regarding such meetings.

Write the managerial style beside the manager's comment to which it applies:

(i)   1.1 Impoverished
(ii)   1.9 Country Club
(iii)   9.1 Task Orientated
(iv)   5.5 Middle of the road
(v)   9.9 Team

I attend because it is expected. I either go along with the majority position or avoid expressing my views.

☐

I try to come up with good ideas, and push for a decision as soon as I can get a majority behind me. I don't mind stepping on people if it helps making a sound decision.

☐

I like to be able to support what my boss wants and to recognise the merits of individual effort. When conflict rises, I do a good job of restoring harmony.

☐

18.5 **Match Charles Handy's Gods of Management beside the cultural organisational classification to which it applies.**

(i)   Zeus
(ii)   Apollo
(iii)   Athena
(iv)   Dionysus

Task culture   ☐

Person culture   ☐

Role culture   ☐

Power culture   ☐

18.6 **Aiming to find a 'win-win' solution is an example of which of the following?**

☐   Distributive bargaining
☐   Integrative bargaining
☐   Purposeful persuasion
☐   Conflict resolution

18.7 **Which of the following statements is correct?**

☐ The primary purpose of a balanced scorecard is to create a corporate strategy

☐ Balanced scorecards always report using the same time periods as the financial accounting system

☐ Organisations should use a 'traffic light' system on their balanced scorecard to help them prioritise their activities

☐ The primary purpose of a balanced scorecard is to increase the number of performance indicators used to manage the business

18.8 **Write Lewin's stage of the change process beside the activities to which it applies.**

(i) Unfreeze
(ii) Change
(iii) Refreeze

Identifying those forces resisting change.

Staff participation to help create the necessary 'buy in' to the new status quo.

Gradually making the move towards its desired end state.

A significant amount of management time will be spent reinforcing the adoption by staff of the new processes.

Strengthening the position of those forces driving the need for change.

The new state being embedded.

18.9 Project W is a severely time-constrained research project and must be completed to high quality standards.

The project staff all have academic qualifications and a wealth of relevant experience.

They are divided into four specialist teams, each working on separate, complex problems.

Each team is headed by an expert in the relevant field.

The project manager has good experience of the general theoretical background to the work being done but ceased to be involved in practical research some years ago.

Using the Ashridge classification, which management style would you expect to be least useful to the project manager?

☐ Tells
☐ Sells
☐ Consults
☐ Joins

18.10 **Identify the terms that complete this statement from the list below.**

- shareholding
- authority
- interest
- turnover
- power
- profitability

Mendelow proposed classifying stakeholders in terms of their level of [＿＿＿＿＿] in a strategy/project and their [＿＿＿＿＿] to influence it.

Answers to Objective Test questions

1a Introduction to strategy

1a.1   The correct response is: The resource-based approach

The positioning approach is used by a company that seeks to identify a gap in the market and fill it.

The outside-in approach is another way of describing the positioning approach.

The ecological approach is the consideration of ecological factors as part of the strategy setting process.

1a.2   The correct answer is: Human resource management, marketing and sales, service.

Human resource management ensures people with the right skills and disposition are hired to work for Sabrina Airways.

Marketing and sales activities ensure that Sabrina Airways understands what the customer wants and that customers are aware of how the business meets their needs.

Service relates to all aspects of the organisation both during and after the delivery of the service eg, in-flight service or dealing with queries prior to or post flight.

Technology development is incorrect because it refers to the technology used to deliver the service, which is not mentioned in the scenario.

Outbound logistics is incorrect because it refers to delivering goods to where the customer can obtain them. This question refers to the delivery of a service.

Firm infrastructure refers to how the business is structured eg, functional, matrix. It can also refer to things like quality assurance processes, so you may have thought this was relevant. 'Service' is a better answer in this case because the scenario relates to a service industry that is people-intensive.

1a.3   The correct answer is: Threshold competences

'Competences' refers to a business' activities or processes. Threshold competences are the absolute basics a company must have to operate. They are not a source of competitive advantage. Core competences on the other hand **are** the company's source of competitive advantage.

'Resources' refers to the things a business has as opposed to what it does (the competences). Resources can also be either threshold or core.

1a.4   The correct answers are:

- Decisions to enter new markets
- Complex decisions
- Relations with external stakeholders

These are all strategically important items which impact the firm as a whole so need to be made at the highest level of the organisation.

Marketing decisions on price will be more appropriately made at Strategic Business Unit level.

Production and distribution decisions should either be made at SBU level or operational level.

1a.5   The correct answers are:

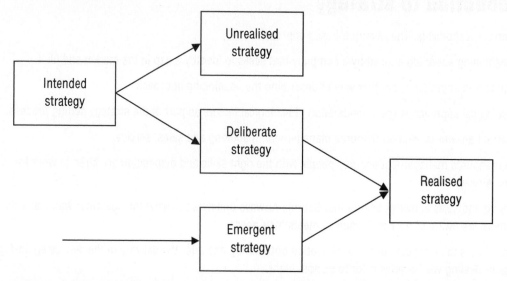

Emergent Strategy starts out the same way as Rational Planning, with an intended strategy. The strategies that are not taken forward are 'unrealised'. Those strategies that are taken forward are 'deliberate' strategies. 'Emergent' strategies are those which are not planned for and incorporated as the deliberate strategy is implemented. Emergent plus deliberate strategies are referred to as 'realised'.

1a.6   The correct answers are:

- Visionary entrepreneurs
- A response to unexpected contingencies
- Strategy can be tried and tested as it is implemented

The key point around emergent strategy is that it develops over time – there is flexibility in the strategy so that if something is not working it is scrapped and if a good idea is suggested it can be implemented.

The other options are features of formal strategy.

1a.7   The correct answers are:

Strength	Weakness
Excellent product design	Over reliance on external providers of quality raw materials
Opportunity	**Threat**
Global economic recovery	Political risk in a country where HKG exports to

1a.8   The correct answers are:

Definition	Insert correct 'P'
Strategy is a unique way of perceiving the world, interpreting information and judging opportunities and choices. Different organisations might respond to environmental stimulus in different ways.	Perspective
Strategy involves manoeuvres to outclass competitors and can be viewed as a competitive business game.	Ploy

1a.9 The correct answers are:

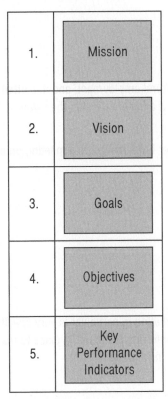

1.	Mission
2.	Vision
3.	Goals
4.	Objectives
5.	Key Performance Indicators

A company will first set its mission – why does it exist? Then its vision – what should the company look like bearing in mind its mission? Then its goals – what does it what to achieve? Then objectives which are more defined than goals, then KPIs which measure progress toward achieving the objectives.

1a.10 The correct answers are:

- Is outside-in
- Ensures the organisation has a good fit with its environment
- Assumes the future of markets is predictable

The other options are features of the resource-based view.

1b Contemporary perspectives in strategy development

1b.1 The correct answer is: Strategic alliance

A merger is two companies becoming one, working together to grow stronger together.

Outsourcing is the contracting of a third party to perform a business operation.

Network organisations are groups of legally independent businesses that work together to appear larger than they actually are, often via the internet.

1b.2 The correct answers are:

- Transaction cost theory allows distinctive competences to be identified
- Transaction cost theory supports organisational restructuring

It is true that transaction cost theory allows distinctive competences to be identified and it supports organisational restructuring.

IT tends to lower, not **increase**, transaction costs as it allows for the more efficient searching, comparison and monitoring of suppliers.

Increased trust also tends to **reduce** transaction costs. Transaction costs are likely to be considerably lower where an existing relationship of trust exists between the supplier and the customer.

1b.3   The correct answers are:

- Rapid economic growth
- Overall improvement in living standards
- Increasing urbanisation

An emerging economy is more likely to experience a decrease in agricultural employment, and it is often the case that economic equality decreases as the rich increase their wealth at a faster rate than the lower socio-economic classes.

1b.4   The correct answer is: Acquisitions involve one entity subsuming another but a merger is a meeting on equal terms.

1b.5   The correct answers are:

Annual spend on veterinary fees	Economy
Number of cats re-homed this month	Effectiveness
Average cost per animal per week	Efficiency

1b.6   The correct answer is: High transaction costs and low control

This is because these functions are crucial to business success and marketing in particular is very specific to each organisation so cannot be outsourced without a high degree of monitoring being put in place to manage the contract. Control will diminish as the processes are managed by the third party.

1b.7   The correct answers are:

Minimising inputs required to generate outputs	Production
Compliance with legislation, treatment of waste etc.	Environmental auditing
Trace the full life-cycle of the product	Ecological approach
A TQM approach to continuous improvement	Quality
Shadow pricing to quantify environmental consequences	Accounting
Environmental cost allocated to relevant processes	Economic

1b.8   The correct answer is: Legislation to make it easier to hire and fire employees.

This makes employment (which supports a traditional organisational structure) more flexible. It would therefore detract from Ghoshal & Bartlett's suggestion.

1b.9   The correct answer is: Licensing

A licensee has the right to manufacture a patented product in return for a fee. It is not a franchising arrangement because Company IEO has the right to market it under its own brand.

1b.10   The correct answers are:

An emphasis on customising products and services to fit local conditions	glocalisation
Functional integration of internationally dispersed activities	globalisation
Extension of trade beyond national/economic/political boundaries	internationalisation

2 General environment

2.1   The correct answers are:

- High level of differentiation, meaning a new competitor will need a differentiated rather than a generic product in order to compete

- High entry costs, meaning a new competitor will need a lot of capital

- Strong brand presence, meaning customers may be loyal to existing firms

- Highly vertically integrated firms, meaning strong supplier/customer relationships which take time to develop

The other items create low barriers to entry.

2.2   The correct answers are:

Power of suppliers	Low
Barriers to entry	High

Supplier power is low because TWS is such an important customer.

Barriers to entry are high because a lot of capital is needed to set up a supermarket.

2.3   The correct answers are:

Control of the money supply	Monetary policy
Interest rates	Monetary policy
Government spending	Fiscal policy
Exchange rates	Monetary policy
Government borrowing	Fiscal policy

Fiscal policy refers to the use of taxation and government spending in order to manage the economy and achieve the government's economic objectives. Monetary policy attempts to achieve the same end but does it through the control of the money supply in the economy.

2.4   The correct answers are:

- Changes in leisure pursuits
- Analysis of the population by age group
- Religious affiliation and practices

The seven categories of the LoNGPEST model are not sealed off from one another and some basic environmental issues may be relevant to more than one category. For example unemployment is an important economic variable but is likely to have effects on people's attitudes and behaviour, so it has social and political implications. Similarly legislation can affect economic and social activity.

2.5   The correct answers are:

Higher education system	Advanced factor
Up to date telecommunications networks	Advanced factor
Access to diverse coastline and complex river systems	Basic factor
Access to road and rail systems	Advanced factor

Basic factors are naturally occurring and require little investment whereas advanced factors are man-made.

2.6   The correct answers are:

- Video conferencing
- High-speed international train link

A substitute product is one that satisfies the same need (facilitating speedy business meetings) but is made or delivered in a different way. The other options are all competitors.

2.7   The correct answer is: Related and supporting industries

One successful industry may lead to advantage in related and supporting industries. At a regional rather than national level, this can also lead to the importance of clusters of organisations from the same industry or sector in the same location within countries.

2.8   The correct answer is: Elimination of business risk due to geographical diversification

Although risk may be reduced it cannot be totally eliminated. The remaining options are benefits of globalisation.

2.9   The correct answer is:

Trigger	Impact
The company's products are successfully differentiated through branding	Increase bargaining power of the seller
The company's customers are signed up to long-term contracts and must pay a penalty if they terminate the contract early	Increase bargaining power of the seller
The company's suppliers are signed up to long-term contracts and must pay a penalty if they terminate the contract early	No impact
There has been a trend toward mergers between the company's customers	Decrease bargaining power of the seller

Differentiation makes it more difficult for customers to transfer to the company's competitors. If customers are tied into long-term contracts protected by penalty clauses, this too represents a switching cost for customers so makes the bargaining power of the company stronger. The same is not true, however, if the suppliers are tied into the long-term contract. Mergers among the company's customer base reduces the number of customers, each buying a larger volume.

2.10   The correct answers are:

- Increase in patent protection
- Requirement for firms in the industry to invest in land and computers

Increases in patent protection and the requirement to invest capital both make entry into an industry more expensive and therefore are barriers to entry. On the other hand the other options may serve to reduce those barriers.

3 Competitive environment

3.1   The correct answers are:

- A focus on 'why' questions rather than 'what' 'where' and 'when
- Costly to undertake
- The attempt to find out customer preferences for our company's products rather than our competitors'

Qualitative research attempts to understand customer preferences rather than simply know what they are and as such, more time and effort will need to be put into gathering the research so it will cost more.

Non-financial data can still be quantitative, and selection of data to analyse is the next step in the process, once data has been gathered - whether it be qualitative or quantitative.

3.2   The correct answers are:

- It helps managers to understand their company's competitive advantages/disadvantages as compared with competitors.

- It aids understanding of competitors' past, present and future behaviour.

- It provides an informed basis to assist a company to develop its own competitive strategies.

Copying a competitor's strategy would not lead to competitive advantage, and analysing a competitor in one industry would not be likely to engender success in a different industry.

3.3   The correct answers are:

Firms whose products satisfy the same needs although they are technically quite different	Form
Firms who compete for the same income, but offer different products	Generic
Firms who have similar products, the same customers and are of a similar size	Brand
Firms who produce similar products but who are different in size or structure or compete in a more limited area/product range	Industry

3.4   The correct answers are:

Selling the same alarms, albeit with different casings, to smaller, less affluent households for a lower price.	Market development
Development of new, more sophisticated alarms and a wide range of security services (guards and surveillance) for sale to industrial clients for higher prices.	Diversification

3.5   The correct answer is:

Cost leadership strategies involve striving to be the lowest price seller in the industry as a whole.	False
According to Porter a cost leadership strategy may be successfully pursued in conjunction with a focus strategy.	True
According to Porter a cost leadership strategy may be successfully pursued in conjunction with one of differentiation.	False

- False – Cost leadership involves being the lowest cost provider (regardless of selling price)

- True – Focus involves segmentation of the market and pursuing either a cost leadership or a differentiation strategy within that one segment.

- False – Porter argues that an organisation should pursue either a cost leadership strategy or a differentiation strategy, otherwise being stuck in the middle will lead to loss of competitive advantage.

3.6   The correct answer is:

The firm reacts strongly to certain types of competitive attacks	Selective
The firm does not remain quiet and reacts strongly to any attack on its markets or products	Tiger
The firm does not exhibit any predictable reaction pattern	Stochastic

3.7   The correct answer is:

- VTT operates in a limited geographical area. For many years there was no significant competition. Recently a new competitor, FID, has been established delivering the same service as VTT. FID is smaller than VTT but has discounted its prices significantly on a number of occasions in its first year. VTT cut its prices just as significantly each time and responded with a vibrant marketing campaign.

  VTT and FID are **industry** level competitors and VTT shows itself to be a **tiger** competitor in reaction to the competitive threat.

Industry (same products but different size and structure)

Tiger (strong reaction to an attack on its market or product)

3.8   The correct answer is:

Big data is a term used to describe the extraction of meaning from vast quantities of **uncorrelated** data. Organisations are particularly interested in identifying **trends** and correlations in the data that they collect and store with the aim of putting this to commercial use.

3.9   The correct answers are:

- Lions
- Silos

Dogs have low market growth and low relative market share.

Cash cows have low market growth but high relative market share.

Question marks are the same as problem children and they have low relative market share but high market growth.

Stars have both high market share and high market growth.

3.10   The correct answer is:

The process of gathering external information which is available from a wide range of sources.	Environmental scanning
What an organisation needs to know about its business environment to enable it to anticipate change and design appropriate strategies that will create business value for customers	Strategic intelligence
Collection and analysis of non-numerical data	Qualitative research

4a Key concepts in management

4a.1   The correct answer is: Awareness of the importance of group dynamics and worker attitudes as an influence on productivity.

Productivity and efficiency are not central concerns of human relations: rather, this could apply to the scientific management school.

Awareness of the variables affecting a manager is a contribution of the contingency school.

Proof of a link between job satisfaction, worker motivation and business success has not yet been provided by any school of management or motivation theory: apart from anything else, business success depends on factors other than the productivity of the workers.

4a.2   The correct answer is: Monitor.

The monitor role involves scanning the environment and gathering information from a network of contacts.

As spokesperson, the manager can then provide information on behalf of the department or organisation to interested parties. A disseminator, can also spread relevant information to team members. The role of leader means hiring, firing and training staff.

4a.3   The correct answers are:

- The job of measurement
- Motivating
- Developing people

Managing a business and managing managers were part of Mintzberg's theory on the role of managers.

4a.4   The correct answers are:

- An airline
- A small retail store
- A design agency

A large accountancy practice will need to ensure it always has the required expertise in-house.

A sports team will need to work hard to foster team spirit at all times, the shamrock does not allow for this.

A sole trader will probably need to be all elements of the shamrock all the time.

4a.5   The correct answers are:

- Targets set are measurable
- Continual review of results
- Staff jointly set objectives with managers
- Goals are stated in behavioural terms

The other responses are likely to result in an ineffective MBO process.

4a.6   The correct answer is: Figurehead.

Interpersonal roles are based on the manager's formal authority: they include the roles of figurehead, leader and liaison. Informational roles are based on the manager's position in internal and external information networks: they include monitor, spokesperson and disseminator.

Decisional roles relate to the work of the manager's department: entrepreneur, disturbance-handler, resource allocator and negotiator.

4a.7   The correct answers are:

At WPW there were small, integrated work groups consisting of a skilled man, his mate and one or two labourers. There was a high degree of autonomy at the work group level. The group was paid for its work as a group.	Social Systems
WPW then introduced new technology creating a need for larger, more specialised groups. A single cycle of mechanised production might extend over three shifts, each performing a separate process and made up of 10 to 20 men. Physical dispersion also greatly increased.	Technical Systems

4a.8   The correct answers are:

Flexible and adaptive organisational forms	Organic Organisations
Stable and efficient organisational forms	Mechanistic Organisations
Suitable for slow-changing operating environments	Mechanistic Organisations
Suitable for dynamic operating environments	Organic Organisations

4a.9 The correct answers are:

- They are ideal for standardised, routine tasks.

- Some people are suited to the structured, predictable environment.

- Rigid adherence to procedures may be necessary for fairness, adherence to the law, safety and security.

The fact that communication is only through suggested channels actually decreases the amount of suggestions made, and bureaucracies do not enhance creativity due to the level of control present. Decisions are made slowly.

4a.10 The correct answers are:

- Unpleasant working conditions
- Below market rate salary
- High levels of supervision and tight control

Other hygiene factors concern policies and procedures and social interaction.

The other factors in the list are motivators.

4b Key concepts in leadership

4b.1 The correct answers are:

The technostructure can undermine the line managers' authority, by empire building:	Clear demarcations of line, staff and functional authority should be created.
Lack of seniority. Middle line managers may be more senior in the hierarchy than technostructure advisers:	Use functional authority (via policies and procedures). Experts should be seen as a resource, not a threat.
Expert managers may lack realism, going for technically perfect but commercially impractical solutions:	Technostructure planners should be fully aware of operational issues, and communicate regularly with the middle line.
Technostructure experts lack responsibility for the success of their ideas:	Technostructure experts should be involved in implementing their suggestions and share accountability for outcomes.

4b.2 The correct answer is:

Delegation is the process whereby a manager assigns part of his **authority** to a subordinate but the manager's **responsibility** can never be delegated.

Authority is defined as the right to do something or ask someone else to do it.

Responsibility is the obligation a person has to fulfil a task they have been given

4b.3 The correct answer is: Referent

Referent power is the power that a person has because they are well liked.

Coercive power is the power a person has to assign punishment.

Reward power is the power a person has to confer rewards.

Expert power is the power a person has who is perceived to have expert knowledge.

BPP
LEARNING MEDIA

4b.4   The correct answers are:

- Knowledge workers
- Flexibility
- Delegation
- Delayering

Centralisation, increasing middle management and top-down management are all things that would decrease empowerment.

4b.5   The correct answer is: Transformational.

Transactional is simply incorrect.

Theory X and Contingency are terms which refer to management rather than leadership.

A key feature of an entrepreneurial leader is creativity, and trait theory considers personal characteristics such as height and intelligence.

4b.6   The correct answers are:

- Managers are freed up to concentrate on higher-level tasks (such as recipe development).

- Delegation shortens the chain of decision making, and brings decisions closer to the situations that require them (which should result in better quality decisions).

- Delegating authority contributes to the job satisfaction and development of the managers who delegate.

The other statements are reasons why delegation might be necessary, except for this statement 'Delegation reduces the need for management to control the performance of staff as they perform more tasks themselves' which is just incorrect.

4b.7   The correct answers are:

Based on analysing the personality characteristics or preferences of successful leaders.	Trait theories
Based on the view that leadership is an interpersonal process whereby different leader behaviours influence people in different ways. More or less effective patterns of behaviour (or 'styles') can therefore be adopted.	Style theories
Based on the belief that there is no 'one best way' of leading, but that effective leaders adapt their behaviour to specific and changing variables in the leadership context: the nature of the task, the personalities of team members, the organisation culture and so on.	Contingency theories

4b.8   The correct answers are

Step 1   Specify performance in terms of the goals and standards expected of the subordinate, keeping in mind their level of expertise.

Step 2   Formally assign tasks to the subordinate, who should formally agree to do them.

Step 3   Allocate resources and authority to the subordinate to enable them to carry out the delegated tasks at the expected level of performance.

Step 4   Back off and allow the subordinate to perform the delegated tasks.

Step 5   Maintain contact, to review progress made, make constructive criticism and be available to give help and advice if requested

4b.9   The correct answers are:

Authority arising from the personality of the leader and their ability to inspire devotion through, for example, sanctity, heroism or example.	Charismatic authority
Authority resting on established belief in the importance of immemorial tradition and the status it confers.	Traditional authority
Authority arising from the working of accepted normative rules, such as are found in organisations and democratic governments.	Rational-legal authority

4b.10 The correct answers are:

This can lead to arbitrary and irresponsible behaviour, as the person has the right to make decisions without being held accountable for them.	Authority without responsibility
This places a subordinate in an impossible and stressful position, as they are held accountable for results over which they have no control.	Responsibility without authority

5 Culture

5.1   The correct answers are:

A large bread company exists in a stable environment, and its structure is well integrated. Management are preoccupied with efficiency with formal ways of behaviour.	Consistency culture
Hospitals are preoccupied with the sick, inevitably their values are patient orientated and staff's work has meaning and value.	Mission culture

Involvement culture satisfies the individual's needs so that they give more to the organisation and the whole becomes more than just the sum of its parts.

Adaptability culture is where a company focuses on its environment and as a consequence, is continually changing.

5.2   The correct answers are:

- Dress codes
- Office layout
- Logos and branding

'Artefacts' are 'concrete expressions' and include the above, but also literature and role models.

5.3   The correct answers are:

- Long-term employment, with slow progressing managerial career paths.
- Collective consensus decision-making processes.
- Industrial relations characterised by trust, co-operation and mutual adjustment.

Theory J states that control is implicit rather than explicit, and that because employees stay with the company for such a long time, they become 'part of the family' so that concern for the employee's well-being stretches beyond the organisational boundary.

5.4   The correct answer is: Process culture.

A process culture focuses on managing risk and 'getting it right'. Don't be led astray by what you perceive a company's culture to be. In order to answer this question correctly you must focus on what the company is meant to do!

5.5 The correct answers are:

You might have to set up team-working in customer-facing units to increase responsiveness.	Structure
You may need to train people in customer service skills.	Skills
They will also need new procedures and IT systems for better access to customer data.	Systems
Managers will have to adjust to empowering staff, and new corporate image will be developed.	Style

'Staff' refers to the number of people in the organisation and 'shared values' refers to the underlying beliefs and assumptions held by the organisation.

5.6 The correct answer is: Individualism.

In this type of culture, where there is low collectivism there must be high individualism.

5.7 The correct answers are:

- Short-term employment with focus on specialisation of skills.
- Individuals ultimately responsible for defined areas of accountability.

Theory A states that concern for employees is related solely to their performance at work, control is explicit and industrial relations are formal, demarcated by the organisation's hierarchy, and feature trade unions heavily.

5.8 The correct answers are:

- Willingness to take risk
- Speed of feedback

The other factors are items that have been considered by other theorists so are plausible, but were not central to Deal & Kennedy's theory.

5.9 The correct answers are:

This exists in a stable environment, and its structure is well integrated. Management are preoccupied with efficiency. Such cultures are characterised by formal ways of behaviour. Predictability and reliability are valued.	Consistency culture
The environment is relatively stable, and the organisation is orientated towards it e.g. 'the customers'. Members' work activities are given meaning and value.	Mission culture
The basic premise is that the satisfaction of employees' needs is necessary for them to provide optimum performance. They take a 'human relations' approach to management.	Involvement culture
The company's strategic focus is on the external environment, which is in a state of change. Corporate values encourage inquisitiveness and interest in the external environment.	Adaptability culture

5.10 The correct answer is: The culture that extends across national boundaries.

The other responses are all distractors.

6 Conflict, negotiation and communication

6.1   The correct answers are:

- They increase management control
- They can provide a fair basis for remuneration
- They enable succession planning

Appraisals increase management control because the appraisal process involves setting targets which are cascaded through the organisation, and progress against these targets is monitored.

Appraisals provide support for cases where a pay rise may be in order, and because they are organisation-wide, the HR department can use them to ensure that staff at a particular grade have a similar skill set and are remunerated on that basis.

Appraisals are also the employee's chance to indicate where they would like to progress in the organisation so that this can be built in to their development plan, or they can be used by management to assess a candidate's readiness to move on.

Because the appraisal is conducted by a person (or people), it is unlikely that it will be 100% objective. Appraisals do not form part of the disciplinary process.

6.2   The correct answers are:

- The company image is protected from a poor health and safety record
- The morale of employees and others is improved
- The legal obligations for health and safety are met

Employees who break health and safety rules do not necessarily need 'punishment' but potentially re-education. The organisation may have guidelines on the consequences of rule breaking but this is not necessarily a 'control'.

Managers (and other employees) will still need to monitor for potential hazards no matter how many controls are in place.

6.3   The correct answers are:

- The choice of words provokes an emotional response
- The filtering out of elements that her or she does not want to deal with
- Limiting the encoding/decoding capabilities of the sender/receiver

Where the choice of words provoke an emotional response that may hinder the receiver from receiving the message clearly.

The other two responses will aid communication.

6.4   The choice of medium will be affected by:

- Permanency: the need for a written record for legal evidence, confirmation of a transaction for future reference.

- Complexity: for example the need for a graphic illustration to explain concepts.

- Urgency: the speed of transition.

In addition, the choice of medium is also affected by the sensitivity/confidentiality of the message, the ease of dissemination and the cost effectiveness of the communication method.

6.5 The correct answers are:

- Published statistics relating to market pay rates.

- Examples of work she has performed to a high standard.

- Details of a client which represents significant financial benefit to J's company that was obtained as a result of J's work.

Market rates of pay and details of J's own work and contribution are all relevant and should be used by J to help her secure a pay rise.

J should not have access to the salary levels of other members of staff and this should not, therefore, be used as part of her negotiations.

It is unclear how J would intend to use the potentially discriminating evidence about her manager's personal life, but this is not relevant to the negotiation and this, nor any other form of bribery, should not be used.

6.6 The correct answer is: Vertical

Vertical conflict is a result of a power imbalance so occurs between different levels of the organisation. Trade unions tend to get involved in this type of conflict most often.

Horizontal conflict occurs between different departments in the organisation.

Diagonal conflict is a combination of vertical and horizontal.

Intergroup is similar to horizontal in that it occurs between people at the same level of the organisation, but conflicting parties can be in the same department.

6.7 The correct answers are:

- The setting of criteria for the selection and career advancement of all staff

- Encouraging flexibility in the treatment of all employees irrespective of their gender, race, age, disability, sexual orientation, religion or political affiliation

- Training managers in fair appraisal methods

Legislation must be followed regardless of whether it is 'supported' by the firm in question.

Just because an organisation claims something in its mission statement does not necessarily mean that it practices what it preaches.

6.8 The correct answers are:

- Fred discussing his grievance with a staff representative
- Abi retracting her threat of suspension
- Abi reporting the situation to her superior

It does not sound as though Abi has grounds to suspend Fred so this position may not be legally supportable. Likewise, it would not be appropriate for Fred to report Abi to the relevant professional body at this stage.

6.9 The correct answers are:

- They spend more time asking questions
- They spend more time checking that they understand what the other party is saying
- They spend more time summarising what is being said

Making a lot of counter-proposals and justifications may make the other party in the negotiation feel like they are not being heard/considered and hinder the negotiation process as a consequence.

6.10 The correct answers are:

Outcomes	Conflict handling strategies
Additional conflict will occur with damage to the organisation and to one or both parties	Competition
A win, win situation	Collaboration
Suppression of interests will result in one party losing out and difficulties may still remain	Accommodation
Lack of effort to deal with causes of the conflict will mean that conflict is likely to recur	Avoidance
Both parties lose out and there may be a better solution if an alternative approach was taken	Compromise

7 Control and the finance function

7.1 The correct answer is:

Market control is the use of the **price mechanism** and related **performance measures**, internally and externally to control organisational behaviours. It is appropriate for use in **loose** organisational forms such as consortia and alliances.

7.2 The correct answer is:

The finance function has faced pressures to become more **actively** involved in business **operations**.

Many finance functions have therefore re-focused their roles as business **partners**, adopting a more **commercial**, action orientated approach.

7.3 The correct answers are:

- The finance function should add value to the organisation
- Actual performance should be rigorously reviewed by the finance function
- The finance function should challenge any results that are better than expected

The finance function should seek to add, but not create value.

The creation of strategy, ideas and opportunities is the responsibility of operational departments, not of the finance function. Finance has a role in the assessment and validation of these ideas, rather than in their creation.

Actual performance should be rigorously reviewed by the finance function and any deviation from the expected results should be challenged. This includes challenging better, as well as worse, performance in order to minimise the risk of understatement.

7.4 The correct answers are:

The payroll process	Outsource
Delivery of the finished products to the customer	Outsource
Customer consultation and bespoke design of furniture	In-house
Build and manufacture of the furniture	In-house
IT support services	Outsource

The customer consultation, furniture design and building of the furniture are all related to the core competences of NT company and so should not be outsourced.

Payroll, delivery and IT support, however, are fairly simple and standardised processes that are not of strategic importance to NT company. These processes could easily be outsourced.

7.5   The correct answer is:

- The costs imposed by businesses on other people, not included in the cost of their products and activities

Externalities are the costs imposed by businesses on other people, not included in the costing of their products and activities. For example, it is recognised that industrial pollution is bad for health.

7.6   The correct answers are:

No sharing of knowledge and best practice	Finance function embedded in business area
Lack the required local knowledge	Shared Service Centre
Higher risk of loss of control and quality	Business Process Outsourcing

If the finance function is embedded in a business area they will get to know that business well and make valuable contributions, but will lack opportunities to learn from other finance staff.

If the finance function is based in a SSC they will be able to share knowledge but will find it harder to build valuable relationships with the rest of the business, based on specific local knowledge.

If the finance function is outsourced, the business may find it hard to ensure that quality standards are maintained because they no longer control that process.

7.7   The correct answers are:

Level in control hierarchy	Aspects of control
Strategic	Setting and reviewing the organisational structure
Tactical	Setting of the production budget
Operational	Computerisation of inventory control

At the highest level, the organisational structure is set and reviewed for appropriateness.

At the mid level of the organisation more detailed control is required to manage the Strategic Business Units, such as the setting of budgets.

At the lowest level of the organisation very detailed controls should be in place, such as continual monitoring of inventory levels.

7.8   The correct answers are:

Departments	Manufacturing	Wages	Finance
Management Control Type	Output	Bureaucratic	Clan

This question tests your knowledge of control strategies. Output control refers to the control of the outcomes of processes eg, how much product is made, bureaucratic control to control through rules and procedures, clan control to control through corporate culture and shared behaviours. Personal control is a distractor ie, not a form of control.

7.9   The correct answer is: Day-to-day management of protégées.

A mentor should not be carrying out the day-to-day management of the protégée.

This is the role of the line manager.

The mentor should be more knowledgeable than the protégée. They should not be their direct line manager or supervisor.

7.10   The correct answers are:

A professional accountant should be straightforward and honest in all professional and business relationships	Integrity
A professional accountant should not allow bias, conflict of interest or undue influence of others to override professional or business judgments	Objectivity
A professional accountant has a continuing duty to maintain professional knowledge and skill and should act diligently and in accordance with applicable technical and professional standards when providing professional services	Professional competence and due care
A professional accountant should not disclose any information acquired as a result of professional and business relationships without proper and specific authority unless there is a legal or professional right or duty to disclose	Confidentiality
A professional accountant should comply with relevant laws and regulations, and should avoid any action that discredits the profession	Professional behaviour

8 Change management

8.1   The correct answer is:

Adaptation is the most common type of change. It does not require the development of a new paradigm and proceeds step by step. Adaptation is therefore the correct answer.

Reconstruction can also be undertaken within an existing paradigm, but requires rapid and extensive action. It is a common response to a long-term decline in performance.

Evolution is an incremental process that leads to a new paradigm. It may arise from careful analysis and planning or may be the result of learning processes. Its transformational nature may not be obvious while it is taking place.

Revolution is a rapid and wide-ranging response to extreme pressures for change. A long period of strategic drift may lead to a crisis that can only be dealt with in this way. Revolution will be very obvious and is likely to affect most aspects of both what the organisation does and how it does them.

8.2   The correct answers are:

Favourable contexts where	Change strategies
There is a lack of information/analysis	Education & communication
Initiators lack information to change & others have power to resist	Participation & involvement
People resist because of adjustment problems	Facilitation & support
Someone or some group will lose out and where that group has power to resist	Negotiation & agreement
Other facilities fail or are too expensive	Manipulation and co-option
Speed is essential and initiators have high power	Explicit and implicit coercion

8.3   The correct answers are:

- Downward adjustment to symbols of status such as a company car
- Questioning of an individual's frame of reference
- Raising concerns for security

Participation is a very powerful motivator so should not produce resistance to change.

A directive management style is expected and usually appropriate in a hierarchical organisation.

8.4 The correct answers are:

- Ageing of the company's infrastructure
- A new Chief Executive Officer begins work
- Industrial action by the workforce

The above are all internal factors.

A drop in the company's market share could be for any number of reasons eg, competitor action such as releasing a new, superior product.

Likewise a shift in exchange rates could be due to a government changing its monetary policy, or political unrest, or response to political unrest elsewhere.

8.5 The correct answers are:

Forces for change: Commitment of employees to the change

Clear articulation of the vision for the future

Encouragement and support from the top

Forces against change: Bureaucracy

Traditional ways of working

Command and control management style

8.6 The correct answers are:

The nature of change will be: Incremental

The scope of change will be: Transformation

An evolutionary change is where a large amount of change happens, but it is done slowly, step by step.

8.7 The correct answer is: To get others to follow the change willingly.

This is the role of a leader.

To challenge things that are taken for granted. Their appointment also signals the importance of the change process. This is the role of an outsider.

To implement the change. This is the role of middle management.

Translation of the overall change strategy into forms suited to specific local contexts. This is the role of middle management.

To bring a fresh point of view and break down the constraints of the existing paradigm. This is the role of an outsider.

8.8 The correct answer is: Entrenched assumptions and habits of mind.

These must be challenged if change is to be achieved.

Routines are the habitual behaviours that members of the organisation display both internally and externally. These can subvert change efforts rather than help them.

Symbolic processes are visible things which can be used as levers of change. The significance of a given symbol may vary from person to person; this makes their use as a tool of change management difficult.

8.9   The correct answers are:

- High levels of uncertainty – employees may wish to stick to what they know.

- Increase in workload – each employee would have to manage the change as individuals in addition to their normal everyday tasks

- Sense of embarrassment – a change may imply they were not doing a good job previously

- Rapid change – this may mean that employees have no time to understand what is happening or prepare

- Loss of autonomy – being 'forced' into changing something without being consulted may leave employees feeling helpless

- Lack skills and competence – this may mean that employees are simply unable to effect the change.

8.10   The correct answers are:

- Attention to target markets – becoming customer orientated.
- Communication with stakeholders – to gain key stakeholder support.
- Crisis stabilisation – using measures to increase revenue and reduce costs.

Consistent financial structure is not needed here because financial restructure is actually usually what is needed to provide cash for investment.

Maintaining the same management team would not help a business turnaround as it is likely that new managers will be required with experience of turnaround and other paradigms.

9 Introduction to project management

9.1   The correct answer is: Increase resources and maintain quality.

Of course, the above is based on an ideal scenario where more resources are available. In real life this is unlikely to be the case.

It will be hard to maintain or increase quality if resources are reduced, and there is no need to increase quality.

9.2   The correct answer is: Managing stage boundaries.

This stage ensures that one stage is properly completed before the next one begins.

Initiation is the stage where scope and objectives are agreed.

Managing product delivery ensures that work done by specialists is completed to the proper standard.

Project assurance is a distractor.

9.3   The correct answer is: 3 days

If the earliest start time is 5 days and the latest finish time is 22 days, you have 17 days in which to complete the project (22-5). If the work takes 14 days, that means you have 3 days spare (17-14).

9.4   The correct answer is: Reduce

This will decrease the instances of the risk occuring. Even if the impact of the risk is not large, it will consume resources if it keeps happening.

Transference is appropriate where a risk cannot be reduced and will have a significant impact on the project.

Avoidance is appropriate if Bethan can take steps to stop the risk from occuring at all.

Acceptance is appropriate where a risk will only have a small impact on the business and cannot realistically be managed.

9.5   The correct answers are:

Activity	Stage in Project Lifecycle
Project Feasibility	Initiation
Testing	Execution
Identifying project risk	Initiation
Audit of deliverables	Project closure
Setting milestones and control gates	Planning
Specifying project scope	Initiation
Cost breakdown structure	Planning
Exception reporting	Execution

At the initiation stage, the project manager will be concerned with setting scope and objectives, and getting an initial sense that the project could succeed.

At the planning stage the detailed planning work will be done in terms of specific activities and what order they should be done in, plus detailed costing.

At the execution phase the project manager will be controlling the project, trying to keep it on track.

At the closing phase, the project manager will be looking to see that the project was completed on time and within budget, and to see what lessons can be taken forward.

9.6   The correct answers are:

- PERT
- Buffering
- Scenario Planning

PERT assesses how much work is done in comparison with how much work is remaining.

Buffering is building in slack time in order to ensure that a project finishes 'on time' if there is slippage.

Scenario planning helps the project manager know what to do should any of a number of different scenarios arise – including slippage.

Financial and economic feasibilty could reasonably be considered similar – concerning the profitability of the project rather than its timescales.

SWOT analysis relates to strategic management.

Work breakdown structure is about the activities that need to take place during the project, not necessarily their duration.

9.7   The correct answers are:

	Type of feasibility
How will waste products be disposed of safely?	Ecological feasibility
How much disruption will the building of the plant cause?	Social feasibility
What is the likelihood of the local community objecting to the project?	Social feasibility
Are the manufacturing processes and equipment available?	Technical feasibility
What pollution could be caused by the project?	Ecological feasibility
What is included in the costs of the project?	Economic feasibility

Ecological feasibility concerns a company's impact on its environment, social feasibility the impact of a strategy/project on its stakeholders, technical feasibility whether something is possible at all, and economic feasibility, financial considerations such as costs and profitability.

9.8 The correct answer is: True.

If these times are different, that means that slack has been added to the end of the project and the team could waste time before signing off.

9.9 The correct answers are:

Network Analysis   is used to analyse the interrelationship between project tasks

Buffering   incorporates risk by adding in slack into risky activities

PERT   assists with risk in project time planning

Gantt Charts   are a graphical representation of project activities

9.10 The correct answer is: Duration of critical path is 12 days.

Activity-on-line style

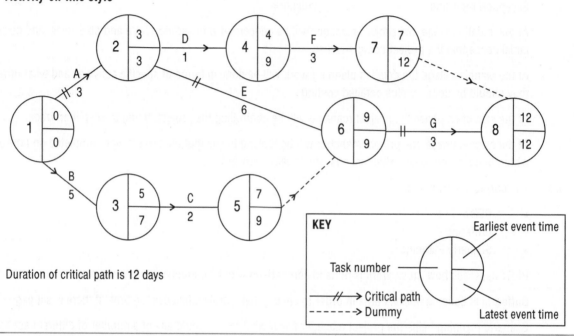

Duration of critical path is 12 days

10 The project team

10.1 The correct answer is: Norming.

At the norming stage there is agreement about work sharing and individual output.

Before the norming stage come the forming and storming stages. The former is characterised by unclear objectives and team members getting to know each other, as well as hesitance to put forward ideas because team member are unsure about others' reactions. The latter is characterised by conflict and possibly changes in previously agreed objectives.

Following the norming stage the members will enter the performing stage, where tasks are being performed competently and efficiently.

10.2 The correct answer is: Forming

When the make-up of the team changes, the team should go back to the forming stage in order for members to get to know each other.

When the task the team is doing changes, the team will go back to the storming stage as they debate how to go about it.

BPP
LEARNING MEDIA

10.3 The correct answers are:

- The Abilene Paradox
- Group think
- Conformity
- Role ambiguity

The other items are benefits of team working.

10.4 The correct answer is: A team has a common purpose, a group does not

A team is defined as 'a small number of people with complementary skills who are committed to a common purpose... for which they hold themselves mutually accountable'.

10.5 The correct answer is: Provides and is accountable for the resources invested in the project.

Communicating the vision of the project within the organisation is the role of the project champion, the project manager is responsible for delivering the project on time; the project board represents the interests of the project sponsor.

10.6 The correct answers are:

- Co-ordinator – controls and organises the group's activities
- Completer/Finisher – chases and ensures deadlines are met
- Team Worker – supports other team members, diffuses conflict

10.7 The correct answers are:

- Adopt an appropriate leadership style for managing change
- Understand the overall strategic objectives of the project
- Be sensitive to the environmental and organisational contexts of the change

By only using formal means of communication the project manager could make themselves less available and miss opportunities to demonstrate good management skills.

A change driven entirely from the top is lacking participation which is a powerful motivator.

10.8 The correct answers are:

- Coordinates project activities
- Provides leadership for the project team
- Responsible for successful delivery of project objectives

The project plan is approved by the project sponsor who also provides the necessary resources. The project owner initiates the project.

10.9 The correct answer is: Its effect on project team motivation.

Team members may work for individual rewards, rather than contributing to the group, especially since there is a problem offering rewards for less measurable criteria such as team-work.

Communication is impacted by PRP because senior management will have to set targets in line with the organisation's key objectives, so they will have to communicate these across the organisation so that employees can understand what they are working hard for.

You may have hesitated over the option about relating to wage and salary grades, but this is a benefit because PRP is a way of rewarding employees when there is no other way to do so (eg because they have reached the top of the salary/wage range their position is eligible for).

10.10 The correct answer is: Completer – finisher.

They key words in the question were 'keen eye for detail', 'always meets deadlines' and 'reluctant to involve others'. These phrases are typical characteristics of a completer-finisher.

11 Mixed Bank 1

11.1 The correct answers are:

The combination of the internal position audit and the external analysis to produce a SWOT analysis.	Corporate appraisal
Internal failures that hinder the organisation from meeting its goals	Weaknesses
Events or changes in the organisation's environment which are unfavourable to the organisation and need to be guarded against	Threats
Events or changes outside the organisation that could be exploited to the organisation's benefit.	Opportunities

11.2 The correct answer is: Market share.

This is traditionally considered to comprise part of an internal position audit rather than an environmental analysis identifying opportunities and threats.

11.3 The correct answer is: Internal benchmarking.

Competitive benchmarking involves the benchmarking of performance with a direct competitor.

Reverse engineering is an exercise whereby a competitor's product is dismantled to see how it is made.

Functional benchmarking is the benchmarking of functions/processes/departments against the best external performer.

Operational benchmarking is a synonym for functional benchmarking.

11.4 The correct answers are:

- There are differences of status, determined by people's greater expertise and experience.
- The degree of commitment employees have to the goals of the firm and the team is more extensive.
- Corporate culture is a powerful guide to behaviour.

In an organic organisation the business is its people, pay scales will be flexible and procedures are open to interpretation.

11.5 The correct answer is: Masculinity – femininity.

Power-distance refers to response to authority. Individualism-collectivism refers to whether value lies with an individual or with a group. Uncertainty avoidance is about the degree to which change is embraced.

11.6 The correct answers are:

A phone conversation with a client is interrupted as a result of interference on the line.	Noise
Information relating to an organisational restructure is provided on a strictly 'need to know' basis.	Cultural values
The new CEO determines that email will now be used as the primary method of communication to ensure documentary evidence is in place should it be needed. This rule is to be applied to all messages from daily updates, to social events, to key operational messages.	Overload

Noise is physical noise such as people talking around you or interference on a phone line.

Overload is getting too much information.

Cultural values refers to the way things are done in the organisation eg, whether there is open communication and knowledge sharing or whether people are only told what they need to know. A reluctance to give bad feedback/news may be a cultural factor.

Jargon is the use of specialist terminology that others may not understand.

Priorities refers to the business's priorities, the targets set by senior management.

Selective reporting is where subordinates only report key messages upwards to their superiors.

Timing is a problem where information has no immediate use so it is forgotten.

Distortion is where information is 'lost in translation', misinterpreted.

11.7   The correct answer is: Customer.

Pricing is a decision related to customers and the value they perceive the organisation to offer them.

The financial perspective is more concerned with traditional measures such as growth, profitability and shareholder value.

11.8   The correct answer is: Elites relationship.

'Political mechanisms' is the collective term used when attempting to exert influence. It includes manipulation of resources, elites relationships, exploitation of subsystems and symbolic activity. The point is that understanding these factors could be advantageous to someone trying to effect change.

Manipulation of resources: The ability to control the allocation of resources (or even merely to influence their allocation).

Exploitation of subsystems: A power base can be established by building up networks and alliances among those sympathetic to change.

Symbolic activity: Change managers may utilise existing symbols and symbolic activities or challenge them, as appropriate.

11.9   The correct answer is: The overall expected duration of the project is 39 weeks.

BEGH = 10+9+14+6 = 39 weeks

Activity-on-line style

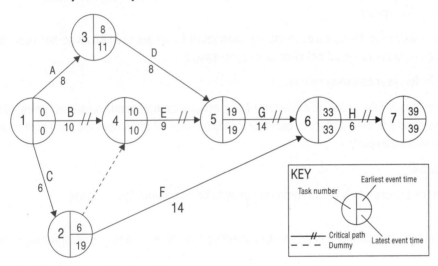

11.10   The correct answer is: Adjourning.

Adjourning is where the group sees itself as having fulfilled its purpose, and there is a process of disconnecting from the task and group – because there will have to be a renegotiation of aims and roles for the new task.

Dorming is where a group grows complacent about performance. Norming is a much earlier stage in the cycle, where the group reaches agreement about work methods, roles and behaviours.

12 Mixed Bank 2

12.1   The correct answer is:

The **positioning** view sees competitive advantage as coming from the way a firm positions itself in relation to its competitors, customers and stakeholders. The **resource-based** view suggests that the organisation should focus on developing a **unique** competence or asset and then find a market which wants it. This is also referred to as an **inside-out view**.

12.2   The correct answer is: Buffering.

Buffering is the lobbying of governments before legislation is ratified in order to explain its potential impact.

Protectionism refers to action taken by one government to restrict trade with others in order to protect their own producers from competition.

Economic liberalisation usually takes the form of the removal of barriers to trade (eg tariffs, quotas, subsidies, tax)

Bridging is the monitoring of political developments so as to ensure compliance with upcoming legislation.

12.3   The correct answer is: Form.

Form competitors aim to satisfy the same need but in different ways. In this case that need is the entertainment of children.

12.4   The correct answer is: Core group.

'Peripheral group' is a distractor. Flexible labour and the contractual fringe are used on an ad-hoc basis and are hired for a specific purpose so would not need to be multi-skilled.

12.5   The correct answer is: Bet your company culture.

This is because the company must make an extremely heavy resource commitment, usually for years, before any benefit of that hard work is seen. Failure to generate significant income after incurring such high costs would mean the end of the company.

12.6   The correct answers are:

A general update on the achievements of the company needs to be communicated to all staff	Email
A product is going to be re-launched and ideas for the marketing campaign need to be generated	Brainstorming session
The payroll manager has become aware of a time-keeping problem with one of the payroll clerks	One-to-one meeting
The organisation is planning a major restructure and the initial plans need to be announced	Large scale meeting
The sales team require an update on their achievements against targets for the last quarter	Team meeting

12.7   The correct answers are:

- To provide good working conditions and decent rewards for all employees.
- To keep employees informed of policy, progress and problems.
- To support the local community and preserve the environment.

By paying a minimum wage to everyone and conforming with legislation, the organisation is fulfilling its legal obligations, not its social responsibility.

12.8 The correct answer is: Evolution.

A change which is an incremental process that leads to a new paradigm. It may arise from careful analysis and planning or may be the result of learning processes. BAMM is planning to change dramatically but over a number of years, so its transformational nature may not be obvious while it is taking place.

12.9 The correct answer is: 12 weeks are needed for the critical path B-F-H.

Activity-on-line style

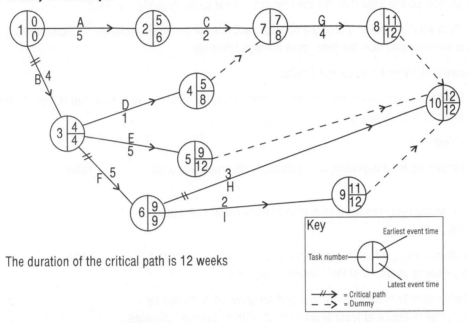

The duration of the critical path is 12 weeks

12.10 The correct answer is: Shaper.

The Shaper is the 'dynamo' of the team: one of the forms of leadership in Belbin's model.

The Plant is the ideas person and creative problem-solver.

The Co-ordinator is the chairperson, clarifying goals, delegating, promoting decision-making. The Implementer is the person who turns ideas into practical actions.

13 Mixed Bank 3

13.1 The correct answer is: Factors fundamental to strategic success.

There is little point in being good at something if it doesn't add value to your business.

13.2 The correct answer: Firm strategy, structure and rivalry.

Firm strategy, structure and rivalry poses the question: 'Does the country's culture and management style help or hinder the industry?'

13.3 The correct answer is: High interest, low power.

The stakeholder may not have the power to disrupt the organisation's strategy but by keeping them informed will ensure the organisation's legitimacy remains intact.

13.4 The correct answers are:

Permanently-employed people who represent the distinctive knowledge and competences of the firm. They are qualified professionals, technicians and managers. Their commitment is focused on their work and career within the organisation. — Professional core

Temporary and part-time workers who can be brought in as and when needed, especially to meet peaks in the demand for services. They are crucial in maintaining standards of service, so it is important for the firm not to treat them 'casually'. — Flexible labour

External providers who are able to undertake non-core activities or provide specialist services, more economically than the firm could manage internally. — Contractual fringe

13.5 The correct answer is: Work hard play hard culture.

The types of business where these cultures can be found are low risk and tend to have fun at work as they may involve an element of creativity.

13.6 The correct answers are:

Distributive bargaining is an approach to negotiation concerned with joint problem solving. — False

Distributive bargaining relates to the distribution of finite resources, not joint problem solving.

Conflict resolution aims to reduce resentment and preserve relationships by allowing both parties to obtain all of their desired outcomes. — False

Conflict resolution aims to reduce resentment and preserve relationships by allowing both parties to obtain **at least some**, not all, of their desired outcomes.

Negotiation is a process whereby two parties come together to confer, with a view to concluding a jointly acceptable agreement. — True

13.7 The correct answer is: Intimidation threat.

As F is D's manager, D is likely to feel that there will be consequences to pay if he does not comply by processing the expense claim. D is therefore facing an intimidation threat.

13.8 The correct answer is: Adaptation.

Wholesome will continue its business as usual, but start to offer a new service on top of what it already does. This is the most common type of change. It does not require the development of a new paradigm and proceeds step by step, hence is relatively low risk.

13.9 The correct answer is: Project sponsor.

The project sponsor provides and is accountable for the resources invested into a project and is responsible for the achievement of the project's business objectives.

13.10 The correct answer is: Performing.

The team is executing its task and the team briefing is dealing with progress to date.

14 Mixed Bank 4

14.1 The correct answers are:

- Trade union's membership increases amongst the employees of an organisation

- The IT department recruits more IT specialists to accommodate a company's decision to sell all its products online

- A supplier wins a contract to be sole supplier of one of the company's competitors

These stakeholders all experience an increase in their power because their claim on the organisation's resources have gone up (in the case of the trade union and the IT department) or their use of resources have become more critical (in the case of the supplier).

The shareholder group has increased its interest but not its power.

If a department's budget has been reduced its power is reduced.

14.2 The correct answer is:

The government in the country of Utopica has recently introduced import **quotas** which limit the volume of overseas meat that can be brought into Utopica. They have also made **subsidies** available to domestic meat producers in order to increase the amount of meat produced within the country. This is an example of a **protectionist** policy.

Quotas limit the volume of goods going into or coming out of a country whereas tariffs are forms of tax on the value of the goods.

Subsidies increase production, taxation on production reduces it.

Protectionist policies aim to protect domestic producers.

14.3 The correct answer is:

- Level of interest
- Level of power

The level of knowledge of a stakeholder group and their level within an internal hierarchy may affect its power and interest but they were not proposed by Mendelow in his matrix.

14.4 The correct answers are:

The payroll department of a firm has well-defined tasks such as paying salaries at the end of the month. There is little variation. Controls are needed to ensure processing accuracy and to avoid fraud.	Mechanistic organisational form
The 'creative department' of an advertising agency, employs a number of professional experts such as copywriters, graphic designers and account executives, who work on projects.	Organic organisational form

14.5 The correct answers are:

The guiding set of beliefs, values and assumptions that shape how the organisation sees itself and its purpose.	The paradigm
The 'mythology' of the organisation: tales of successes and failures, how things got to be the way they are.	Stories
Symbolic behaviours such as business formulation and ceremonies, as well as formal procedures and customs.	Rituals and routines
Ways in which control is exercised via standards, monitoring and supervision.	Control systems

14.6 The correct answers are:

After numerous discussions with the potential client, K is intending to secure a deal with the client at this meeting.	Purpose
The potential client has a reputation for being a fierce negotiator and driving hard bargains.	Personalities
As numerous discussions have already been held, few introductions will be required.	Pace
A break-out room will be required for discussions between K and her team at various intervals.	Plan

14.7 The correct answer is:

Companies should have an audit committee consisting of **non-executive** directors, the majority of whom should be **independent**.

The audit committee should **review** the audit, and the independence and objectivity of the **auditors**.

14.8 The correct answer is: Hijacked process of change.

Ritualisation of change is what happens when change programmes extend into the longer term. For example, changes to the NHS (the UK national healthcare system) made with every new government. There is a danger that organisation members will come to view the initiatives as mere ritual with little real significance.

Erosion. This means that the successful introduction of new initiatives may suffer erosion from the effects of other events and processes, as, for example, when high staff turnover hampers staff development.

Reinvention. Recalcitrant staff may reinvent the nature and implications of the change programme in a way that accommodates previous undesirable practices. This is a failure of monitoring and control.

14.9 The correct answers are:

- Teambuilding

  The work is carried out by a team of people often from varied work and social backgrounds. The team must 'gel' quickly and be able to communicate effectively with each other.

- Expected problems

  Expected problems should be avoided by careful design and planning prior to commencement of work.

- Unexpected problems

  There should be mechanisms within the project to enable these problems to be resolved quickly and efficiently.

- Delayed benefit

  There is normally no benefit until the work is finished. The 'lead in' time to this can cause a strain on the eventual recipient who is also faced with increasing expenditure for no immediate benefit.

- Potential for conflict

  Projects often involve several parties with different interests.

  This may lead to conflict.

14.10 The correct answer is: Unity of command.

Matrix organisation is based on dual command: the classical principle of unity of command is 'one person, one boss'.

15 Mixed Bank 5

15.1 The correct answers are:

- Franchising
- Joint ventures
- Consortia
- Licensing

A strategic alliance is the sharing of resources and activities across two or more organisations in order to pursue strategies.

Acquisitions and mergers are not strategic alliances.

Acquisitions are the purchase of one organisation by another.

Merger are where two or more organisations come together to create a single, larger organisation.

15.2 The correct answers are:

- National
- Technological
- Global

LoNGPEST stands for:

- Local
- National
- Global
- Political
- Economic
- Social
- Technological

15.3 The correct answer is: Low market growth.

Cash cows have low market growth and high market share. Dogs have low market share and low market growth.

15.4 The correct answers are:

The leader has only superficial trust in subordinates, motivates by reward and, though sometimes involving others in problem solving, is basically paternalistic.	Benevolent authoritative
The leader imposes decisions, never delegates, motives by threat, has little communication with subordinates and does not encourage teamwork.	Exploitative authoritative
The leader has confidence in subordinates, who are allowed to make decisions for themselves. Motivation is by reward for achieving goals set by participation, and there is a substantial amount of sharing of ideas, opinions and co-operation.	Participative
The leader listens to subordinates but controls decision making, motivates by a level of involvement, and will use the ideas and suggestions of subordinates constructively.	Consultative

15.5 The correct answers are:

Culture is shaped by one individual	Power
Culture is a bureaucratic culture shaped by rationality, rules and procedures	Role
Culture is shaped by a focus on outputs and results	Task
Culture is shaped by the interests of individuals	Person

15.6 The correct answers are:

- They consider a wide range of options
- They use emollient verbal techniques: 'would it be helpful if we...?'
- They summarise on behalf of all involved
- They advance single arguments insistently and avoid long winded, multiple reason arguments

John Hunt also identified the following characteristics of successful negotiators.

- They avoid direct confrontation
- They hold back counter proposals rather than responding immediately

15.7 The correct answer is:

Organisations exist for the benefit of shareholders.

This view rejects the idea that the needs and opinions of other wider stakeholders should be taken into account.

A more progressive view sometimes referred to as the ecology model recognises that the needs and opinions of all stakeholders groups (both financial and non-financial) are valid.

The ecology model recognises that organisations exist within a wider environment and that there are many advantages to be gained from taking this approach.

15.8 The correct answer is: Uncontrolled efforts.

Ivory tower change occurs when change is imposed from the top down; its proponents may be seen as inhabiting an ivory tower, being out of touch with operational reality and lacking in credibility as a result.

Lack of attention to symbols. Occurs when change managers who pay insufficient attention to symbols can both fail to make the change relevant to the employees' day-to day reality and succeed in sending the wrong messages.

Behavioural compliance. Apparent behavioural compliance may disguise lack of commitment. People may appear to comply with the changes, without actually 'buying into' them.

15.9 The correct answer is: Project scope.

A project scope states what is included and what is not in a project.

15.10 The correct answer is: Dual authority.

Dual authority may lead to conflict between the managers involved.

The advantages of such a structure are:

- Greater flexibility
- Improved communications
- Employee motivation

16 Mixed Bank 6

16.1 The correct answer is:

If Company HJJ decides to do its payroll in-house, managers will then focus on monitoring and controlling that function's use and performance. This is known as a **hierarchy** solution. The company may enter into a contract to buy in the payroll services from an external supplier as long as the **transaction** costs associated with this last option are not too high. This option is called the **market** solution.

16.2 The correct answer is: one that meets the same needs but is made or delivered in a different way.

A substitute product is one that meets a similar need to another product or service but it is made and delivered in a different way. For example e-mail is a substitute for physical delivery of letters.

16.3 The correct answers are:

- Market research to ascertain customers' buying attitudes
- Hiring a consultant in order to train employees on new health and safety legislation

The other options are concerned with internal information (eg sales ledger and work patterns) or is informal (eg the chief executive learns the news by chance from his/her spouse).

16.4 The correct answer is: Staff authority.

Staff authority is the authority that a member of one department has to give specialist advice to members of another department, where there is no line authority.

16.5 The correct answer is: Task.

A task culture is focused on getting the job done in the most efficient way possible, and this usually requires the high degree of flexibility that a matrix structure provides.

16.6 The correct answers are:

- Purposeful persuasion
- Constructive compromise

The process of negotiation involves two main elements: purposeful persuasion and constructive compromise.

Conflict resolution and problem solving are examples of situations that negotiation can be applied to.

Distributive bargaining and integrative bargaining are approaches to negotiation.

16.7 The correct answer is: T's mentor.

T's mentor would be ideally placed to guide T on these matters by providing overviews of the organisation and organisation charts and explaining responsibilities of relevant members of staff.

16.8 The correct answers are:

A change which is a rapid and wide-ranging response to extreme pressures for change. A long period of strategic drift may lead to a crisis that can only be dealt with in this way. It will be very obvious and is likely to affect most aspects of both what the organisation does and how it does them.	Revolution
A change undertaken within an existing paradigm, but requiring rapid and extensive action. It is a common response to a long-term decline in performance.	Reconstruction
The most common type of change. It does not require the development of a new paradigm and proceeds step by step.	Adaptation
A change which is an incremental process that leads to a new paradigm. It may arise from careful analysis and planning or may be the result of learning processes. Its transformational nature may not be obvious while it is taking place.	Evolution

16.9 The correct answer is: Feasibility analysis.

This looks at whether a proposed project can achieve its objectives in a cost-effective manner.

16.10 The correct answer is: Keep informed.

Local nature appreciation groups would have high interest (due to potential environmental impacts) but relatively low power: because of their high interest, though, they might be able to band together or lobby to increase their power.

So a 'keep informed' strategy is appropriate to try to prevent them becoming a key player by campaigning to local government representatives or government bodies such as the Environment Agency.

17 Mixed Bank 7

17.1   The correct answers are:

Company A   Franchise – the franchisee manufactures or distributes a product or service while the franchiser retains control of the brand and marketing

Company B   Virtual network – an organisation with few physical assets and relies heavily on IS/IT

Company C   Consortium – short-term legal entity set up to deliver a particular project

17.2   The correct answer is: The government uses import taxes and tariffs to protect developing industries and reduce the country's dependence on foreign imports.

The policy is aimed at making imports less attractive so that the country becomes more self-sufficient in terms of the goods and services it consumes.

17.3   The correct answers are:

- Niche market segments can be more secure.
- The firm does not try to achieve too much with too little early in the business cycle.

The other options are disadvantages of a focus strategy.

17.4   The correct answers are:

The process by which one person modifies the behaviour or attitude of another.	Influence
The term for making workers (and particularly work teams) responsible for achieving, and even setting, work targets, with the freedom to make decisions about how they are to be achieved.	Empowerment power
The right to do something, or to ask someone else to do it and expect it to be done.	Authority

17.5   The correct answers are:

The purpose of the organisation is to serve the interests of the individuals who make it up. Management is directed at facilitating and administering.	Dionysus
The organisation is controlled by a key central figure, owner or founder. Power is direct, personal and informal. Suits small organisations where people get on well.	Zeus
Management is directed at outputs, problems solved and projects completed. Team-based, horizontally-structured, flexible and valuing expertise – to get the job done.	Athena
Classical, rational organisation with bureaucracy. Stable, slow-changing, formalised and impersonal. Authority based on position and function.	Apollo

17.6   The correct answers are:

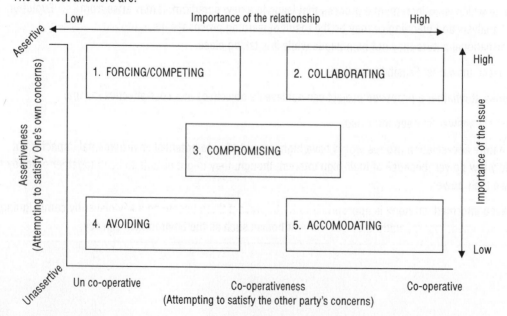

17.7   The correct answers are:

To carry out risk assessments, generally in writing, of all work hazards at least once	False – this should be done on a continual basis
To introduce controls to prevent risks	False – risks can only be reduced, not prevented
To identify employees who are especially at risk	True
To provide information to employees about health and safety	True

17.8   The correct answers are:

- Preservation required
- Diversity of experience
- Capacity to undertake
- Readiness of workforce
- Power to effect

The preservation of some organisational characteristics and resources may be required.

Diversity of general experience, opinion and practice is likely to ease the change process: homogeneity in these factors is unlikely to do so.

Capacity to undertake change depends on the availability of resources, particularly finance, and information systems/information technology (IS/IT), and management time and skill.

The degree of workforce readiness for change will affect its success. Readiness may be contrasted with resistance to change, which can exist at varying levels of intensity and may be widespread or confined to pockets.

The power to effect change may not be sufficient to overcome determined resistance among important stakeholder groups. This can apply even at the strategic apex, where, for example, major shareholders, trustees or government ministers may constrain managers' freedom of action.

The others options are pertinent to change, but not in this context.

17.9   The correct answer is: Initiation.

Project scope is all the things that have to be achieved if the project is to succeed. This should be done at the beginning of the project lifecycle when the project is being initiated.

17.10   The correct answer is: Storming.

This is the storming stage, as identified by Tuckman. During this stage, conflict can be quite open. Objectives and procedures are challenged and risks are taken. However, there is a considerable amount of enthusiasm within the group and new ideas emerge. So too do political conflicts, as leadership of the group becomes an issue. This appears to be the situation described in the question.

18 Mixed Bank 8

18.1   The correct answer is: Contract price.

The contract price is the direct cost of outsourcing the payroll work.

Performance monitoring, tendering contract negotiations and loss of internal skills are all indirect and ongoing costs of the outscoring.

18.2   The correct answers are:

Bridging: Reading newspapers and watching news bulletins, consulting with their legal team, and attending forums. All in order to ensure they are aware of any changes in political direction which may affect them and can respond to them. Bridging is monitoring political developments so as to ensure compliance.

Buffering: Taking their local MP out to lunch and campaigning the Department for Business, Innovation & Skills in order to try to persuade the government not to implement a particular bit of legislation that will impact them negatively. Buffering is lobbying government before legislation is ratified in order to explain its implications.

18.3   The correct answer is:

In the context of the Boston Consulting Group matrix relative market share is assessed as a ratio. It is the market share of one company compared to the market share of the largest competitor providing that same product	True
Exploitation of the learning curve in early stages of production of a new product may help in the pursuit of a cost leadership strategy	True
Where one organisation sells home improvements and another sells package holidays these organisations may be described as form competitors	False

The definition of relative market share is correct.

The learning curve represents cost saving that can be generated because the workforce is getting quicker and more efficient at producing a good, it will therefore help to reduce the organisation's cost base.

The relationship described here is a generic form of competition. Form competitors produce goods and services that are technically different but satisfy the same need.

18.4   The correct answers are:

I attend because it is expected. I either go along with the majority position or avoid expressing my views.	1.1 Impoverished
I try to come up with good ideas, and push for a decision as soon as I can get a majority behind me. I don't mind stepping on people if it helps making a sound decision.	9.1 Task Orientated
I like to be able to support what my boss wants and to recognise the merits of individual effort. When conflict rises, I do a good job of restoring harmony.	1.9 Country Club

18.5   The correct answers are:

Task culture	Athena
Person culture	Dionysus
Role culture	Apollo
Power culture	Zeus

18.6   The correct answer is: Integrative bargaining.

Aiming to find a 'win-win' situation which fulfils the needs of all parties as far as possible is an example of the integrative bargaining approach to negotiation.

The distributive bargaining approach to negotiation is related to the distribution of finite resources.

Purposeful persuasion is where each party attempts to persuade the other to accept its case, conflict resolution aims to reduce resentment and preserve relationships.

18.7   The correct answer is:

- Organisations should use a 'traffic light' system on their balanced scorecard to help them prioritise their activities.

The balanced scorecard is a key tool that organisations can use to help them improve their performance. Consequently a traffic light system can be used to ensure the organisation focuses on areas that are hindering its overall performance.

The balanced scorecard helps the organisation monitor progress towards its strategy rather than helping to create it, and can be reported at any time the organisation requires rather than in line with the financial reporting periods.

Rather than increasing the number of performance indicators used, the balanced scorecard should help to redress the balance between financial and non-financial performance indicators and therefore improve the quality of them. Any subsequent increase will happen as a side-effect rather then being the primary purpose of the balanced scorecard.

18.8   The correct answers are:

Identifying those forces resisting change.	Unfreeze
Staff participation to help create the necessary 'buy in' to the new status quo.	Change
Gradually making the move towards its desired end state.	Change
A significant amount of management time will be spent reinforcing the adoption by staff of the new processes.	Refreeze
Strengthening the position of those forces driving the need for change.	Unfreeze
The new state being embedded.	Refreeze

18.9   The correct answer is: Tells.

This is a tricky question. The characteristics of the project staff are such that a consultative or even democratic style might be recommended. However, the time and quality constraints mean that the project manager is likely to have to exercise firm control on occasion. This would probably be best done in a persuasive style. The conclusion is that the autocratic style will probably be of least use.

18.10   The correct answer is:

Mendelow proposed classifying stakeholders in terms of their level of **interest** in a strategy/project and their **power** to influence it.

BPP
LEARNING MEDIA